Cricut for Beginners

A Beginners Guide to Master your Cricut Machine. Updated and Detailed Step by Step Guide with Project Ideas and Design Space.

Caren Smith

Table of Contents

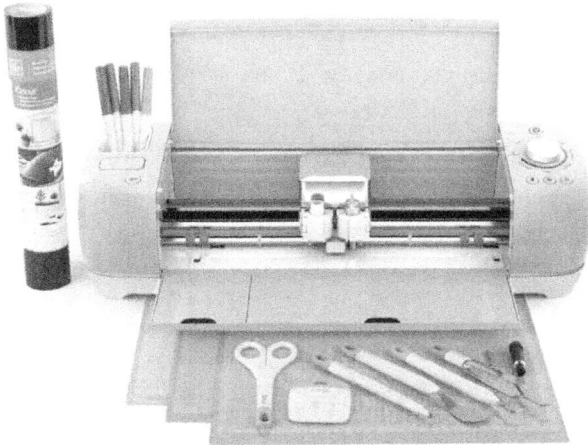

Introduction

Congratulations on downloading *Cricut for Beginners* and thank you for doing so.

The following chapters will discuss everything from choosing the Cricut machine that's right for you and your needs, to creating beautiful projects with a professional, polished appearance. Cricut can assist you to make projects that look so professional, people will want to know where they can buy your products.

Cricut is a smart cutting tool that you can use to create or personalize just about anything you can imagine. We'll give you everything you need to know to get you started, as well as the insider information from the most experienced crafters that use this revolutionary tool!

There are plenty of books on this subject on the market, thanks again for choosing this one! Every effort was made to ensure it is full of as much useful information as possible, please enjoy!

Chapter 1: Getting Acquainted with Cricut

What is Cricut?

The generic title for the Cricut is a die cutter, craft plotter, or a smart cutting machine. The format of this machine allows you to create projects from flat materials of varying thicknesses. The projects that you can do with this tool can range from simple to quite complex, depending on your skill level with these materials. Depending on the sharpness of the blade in your cutting machine, or the model that you're using, your materials can range anywhere from craft felt to thin sheets of metal. This gives you an idea of how vast the range really is, for what this machine can help you to accomplish as a crafter.

Other machines of this type can run you several hundred or even thousands of dollars, require design degrees, come with complex proprietary software, and offer only a fraction of the design options that come with Cricut, and the proprietary, user-friendly Cricut Design Space. Cricut's massive base of users are always sharing the latest and greatest in projects, tips, tricks, guides, and new materials to use with your Cricut machine. As a crafter with a Cricut machine, your resources are nearly limitless.

Thanks to the vast number of resources at our disposal as crafters, I've decided to compile the best of what's available, so you don't have to sift through anything confusing before getting started making your gorgeous projects and loving your new Cricut machine. In one organized place, you'll be able to access all the information you need on how to use the software, project guides that take you from start to finish, a list of all that you will need, and so much more. This is your comprehensive guide that you can refer to again and again, no matter how your skill level grows over time!

I'm intent on bringing you all the most important knowledge on the subject of Cricut, what it can do, how to get the most out of your machine, and how to consistently get the best results. The trade secrets outlined in the later chapters of this book will have you crafting like a professional in no time at all. Feel free to bookmark chapter six of this guide, which will contain all your Frequently Asked Questions, troubleshooting tips, and Cricut Hacks so solutions are always right at your fingertips.

Just like with many other crafting media, if you're not paying attention, it is possible to spend more than you intended on materials, tools, accessories, and more. My intention is to show you which proprietary tools are worth the extra money, while showing you the best alternatives that you can use in place of other tools. Crafting is such a therapeutic and enjoyable experience; it shouldn't be prohibitive thanks to the cost! As you gain familiarity with the community of Cricut users, with the Cricut brand, I'm confident you will find the products and tricks that work the best for you in bringing your crafts to life!

Let's dive into how to choose the right Cricut model for you and for your needs!

How Can I Choose the Right Model for Me?

The wonderful thing about Cricut is that their models are all incredibly versatile and capable. Most capabilities that are had by one model will span the entire current Cricut line of products. There are some very minor differences in the ways in which they work and the complexity of their operation.

In the section below, I've listed all the models that are currently available from Cricut, what they do, how they differ, and what areas are stronger amongst some models.

What's Available?

Thankfully, there is not a vast number of craft plotters available from Cricut at the time of writing, which means it will be really easy for you to take a look at all of what's offered without being overwhelmed. With huge product lines that contain many various models, finding what you want and need, while getting the most for your money can be a real chore. I'll outline each of the models currently available, what they can do, and what capabilities are best suited for what types of crafts.

Cricut Explore One

In terms of what is currently available from Cricut, this is the most basic machine they offer. This machine boasts being able to cut 100 of the most popular materials that are currently available to use with your Cricut machine, as well as being perfectly user friendly.

The Cricut Explore One is considered to be the no-frills beginner model of Cricut craft plotters and operates at a lower speed than the other models available. Unlike the others available in the current product line, the Cricut Explore One has only one accessory clamp inside, so cutting or scoring, and drawing cannot be done simultaneously. They can, however, be done in rapid succession, one right after the other.

While this is a great tool for a wide range of crafts on 100 different materials, and which can get you well on your way to designing breathtaking crafts that are always a cut above others, the cost is not as high as you might imagine. If you intend to use your craft plotter mainly for those special occasions where something handcrafted would be perfect, then this a great machine to have on hand.

At the time of writing this, the cost for the Cricut Explore One is $179.99

Cricut Explore Air

With all the capabilities of the Cricut Explore One and more, the Cricut Explore Air model comes equipped with Bluetooth capability, has a built-in storage cup to keep your tools in one place while you're working, so they won't roll away or get lost in the shuffle.

This model does have two on-board accessory clamps, which allow for simultaneous marking and cutting or scoring. These clamps are marked with an A and a B so you can be sure your tools are going in the right places, every time you load them in.

This model is equipped to handle the same 100 materials as the Cricut Explore One, and operates at the same speed, so the price difference reflects those differences *and* the similarities! This is a great value for the powerhouse that you're getting.

At the time of writing this, the cost for the Cricut Explore Air is $249.99

Cricut Explore Air 2

The Cricut Explore Air 2 is Cricut's current top selling craft plotter and is arguably the best value they have to offer for the price. This model cuts materials at twice the speed of the previous two models, has Bluetooth capability, and has the two on-board accessory clamps.

The storage cup on the top of the machine features a secondary, more shallow cut to store your replacement blade housings when they're not in use, so that if you happen to be swapping between several different tips for a project, they're all readily available to you throughout your project. Both of the cups have a soft silicone bottom, so you won't have to worry about the blades on your machine becoming dull or scratched!

For someone who finds themselves using their Cricut with any regularity, this is the best machine for the job. You will be able to do your crafts twice as fast, and you will get a satisfactory result every time, even at that speed!

At the time of writing, the Cricut Explore Air 2 is priced exactly the same as the Cricut Explore One, at $249.99. If you're looking to jump on this, now is the time to get the best deal.

Cricut Maker

The Cricut Maker is considered to be Cricut's flagship model. This is the one that can do just about anything under the sun on just about any material you can fit into the mat guides of your machine. The one drawback of this powerhouse model is the price point. This does make this model more prohibitive, unless you plan to make crafts that you can sell with this model. If this is your intention, you can rest assured that whatever you turn out with this machine will be the best of the best, every single time. If you're selling your crafts, this baby will pay for itself in little to no time at all.

For the avid crafter who likes to show up to the party with the most gorgeous crafts that are leaps and bounds ahead of their peers, this machine might be overkill for the price. Of course, if you are keeping up with the Joneses, this is the model to have.

This model really does have it all and we can prove it. No other Cricut machine has the speed that the Cricut Maker has. The cuts that can be made with the special precision blades that fit only this machine, are crisper than anything you could ever hope for from a straight knife or other craft cutter. The blade housings allow you to simply remove the tip from the housing, install the next one, clip it back into place, and keep on rolling through your projects. In addition to this, the machine can detect the material loaded into it, so you won't need to set the type of materials at the beginning of each of your projects. With the other model, a common occurrence is that the project is halfway done before the crafter realizes that the dial is set incorrectly.

The machine, like some of the others, is fully Bluetooth capable, it operates with ten times as much power as any of the other models, it has a special rotary cutter attachment that allows it to glide effortlessly through fabrics and precision, and so much more.

At the time of writing, the Cricut Maker is priced at $399.99

Are There Older Models?

In a word, yes. There are several older models that have been phased out to make way for the Explore and Maker machines. The older machines were found to require a good deal more hacks, workarounds, troubleshooting, and understanding to get precise or even rounded cuts for the projects that crafters would like to do.

Here is a list of some of the models you may have seen in your travels:

- Personal Cricut Electronic Cutter Machine
- Cricut Create
- Expression 1
- Expression 2
- Imagine
- Cricut Mini
- Cricut Explore

Each of these models was compatible with a Cricut product called the Gypsy, which was not unlike the Cricut Design Space that we currently have today. Each of these machines had its triumphs in innovating the craft cutting processes.

The major aspect that Cricut aimed for overhauling when creating their newest line of models, was the complexity involved in working with their machinery. Communities of crafters had come together with hacks and math ledgers to program their machinery to work precisely as they wanted it to.

With the current line of available models, the Cricut Design Space allows you to be an innovative as you can possibly be with the design process, so none of your creative flow is eaten up by operations that should be taken care of by your machine.

If you own one of these machines, updating is certainly worth the money, but if it has served you well in your crafting, there is no need to upgrade. Cricut has always made quality products, and the cartridges containing various themed design elements are still supported through Cricut Design Space.

The Cricut Cartridge Adapter is a USB adapter, which allows you to import your cartridges into the Cricut Design Space, so all your elements are available in one organized space.

What are the Tools?

Cricut is a brand that listens to its customers. Thanks to this, they've thought of every possible tool you would need in order to take your project from the very beginning, all the way to completion. I've compiled a list of all the tools that will assist you in bringing your projects out of Cricut Design Space, and into reality.

Take a look through these items, get a feel for what they are, what they do, and you can see some of the ones right off the bat that can be substituted with other tools that aren't part of the Cricut brand.

In doing this, you will save money, and you may be able to make use of some of the tools you currently have around your crafting station! Let's dive in.

Bonded Fabric Blades

These blades are made with German carbide steel to cut through bonded fabric with ease and precision. They should be used with the FabricGrip™ mat, to keep your fabric in place for the most precise, cleanest cuts.

These blades, and the housings that are also available for them, are designed and crafted specifically to fit the Explore line of Cricut cutting machines, including the Explore Air models. The Cricut Maker requires a different type of blade and housing.

Craft Tweezers

These reverse-action tweezers have a strong grip, precise points, and alleviate cramping after prolonged use. The ergonomic grip makes it possible to keep a tight grip on your materials throughout the project, giving you that extra set of hands you always wish you had while crafting.

Cricut Explore® Wireless Bluetooth® Adapter

This product is to help your Cricut Explore machine connect with Bluetooth to your computer or device. If you've invested in the Cricut Explore One, but have found the Bluetooth capabilities to be helpful, this handy adapter makes easy work of adding that capability to your Cricut Explore One machine.

Deep-Point Replacement Blades

Deep-point blades allow you to make deeper, more precise cuts on even thicker materials with ease. Over time, you will find the blades in accessory clamp B will begin to go dull or will simply be less precise. Cricut offers a line of replacement blades to overcome this, and your blades will also respond to sharpening on a couple of occasions before replacement.

Paper Crafting Set

If you're particularly into papercraft, you will find the edge distresser, quilling tool, piercing tool, and craft mat in this set to be essential in your crafting. Quilling or paper filigree art is more popular than ever these days and these are some of the best tools available for that craft.

Portable Trimmer

This is a precision cutting tool that allows you to get fast, crisp, straight cuts on your projects 100% of the time. These are especially popular among scrapbookers, so other versions of this product are largely available on the market, so keep your eye out for ones with great reviews and a low price point.

Replacement Blades

There are replacement blades and housings that are available for every model on the current Cricut line. Any blades that fit the Cricut Explore One will fit any model in the Cricut Explore line. The blades for the Cricut Maker will only fit that specific model, so be sure to check the product descriptions or packaging to ensure you're getting the right blade for you.

Rotary Cutting Kit

This kit comes with a gridded cutting mat and a rotary cutting tool that makes fast, straight, precise cuts every time. Cricut is far from the only brand that offers a rotary cutting tool, so be sure to look at other brands on the market for the tool and price that are best for you.

Scissors

Any crafter knows that scissors are an integral part of their tool kit. While the scissors that Cricut offers are exceedingly sharp, with very fine points on each blade, any pair that is suited for your craft will serve you well here.

Scoring Stylus

The scoring stylus is meant to fit perfectly into accessory clamp A of your machine to score your projects to create and embossed effect, fold lines, and so much more. The tool can also be used freehand to create the effects you'd like to create in your art.

Scraper/Burnishing Tool

This simple tool will be your most-used Cricut tool, with the possible exception of the weeding tool. You will find that once you lift your cut designs from the backing sheet, transferring them to your project surface will require even, steady pressure for burnishing your projects beautifully. This tool, in a pinch, can be replaced with other items, but this tool really does do the best work.

Spatula

Sometimes you feel like you need an extra set of hands when you're peeling or laying down a project. This tool gives you that extra support and maneuverability where you need it.

TrueControl™ Knife

This is a precision blade that is comparable to XACTO in quality and in type. For more precise freehand cuts, this knife is very helpful at any crafting station.

Weeding Tool

This is a hook with a very fine point that allows you to peel blanks from your cut vinyl. This tool will come in handy for most, if not all the projects you do with your Cricut. It helps you to remove your design from the excess material without having to bend, fold, or fight with your material. This helps to keep the edges of your design crisp, clean and sharp every time.

XL Scraper/Burnishing Tool

This provides a level of control that cannot be beat. It exerts pressure evenly and helps to eliminate uneven layering and air bubbles. This tool comes very highly recommended by the community of users.

Paper Crafting Set – If you're particularly into papercraft, you will find the edge distresser, quilling tool, piercing tool, and craft mat in this set to be quite to your liking. Quilling or paper filigree art is gaining popularity these days and these are some of the best tools available for that craft.

Chapter 2: Cricut Design Space

How do I get Started?

The Cricut Design Space Software is an application that is run entirely from the web. This means you will need an active internet connection in order to use it, but downloading the plugin will allow you to jump in and use Cricut Design Space from your device. You can download this plugin onto any laptop or computer, log in with your credentials, and you can have access to your designs from anywhere, so long as you have an active internet connection.

When you first log into the Cricut Design Space, the prompts will ask you what type of Cricut device you'd like to install. This will allow the program to communicate with your device properly and lay out your cuts perfectly. Once you've done this step and your computer has identified the proper device, you'll want to click the "New Project" button in the upper right-hand corner. This is where you'll be prompted to download the installer for the Cricut Design Space Plugin.

Opening the Design Space Plugin Installer for the first time will prompt you to link your device to the Cricut machine. Establishing this connection allows your computer and your Cricut device to communicate seamlessly. Once this connection is established, you'll be able to create projects whenever you'd like. This means you can import images that you have found in other places, images you've created yourself, or you can use the images that Cricut offers either for free or through Cricut's paid Access subscription.

The first thing you need to know about Cricut Access is that *you do not need this subscription to use the Cricut Design Space.* You can make use of every aspect of your Cricut machine without ever signing up for Cricut Access.

The benefits that one gets from a Cricut Access membership varies depending on the subscription tier you choose. At the time of writing, there are three tiers of membership available to the Cricut Access program.

Monthly - $9.99 per month

With the monthly Cricut Access subscription, you are granted the unlimited use of over 400 fonts that are available in the Cricut Design Space, unlimited, unrestricted use of over 90,000 images that you can use for any design in the Cricut Design Space, 10% member savings on purchases from Cricut's website, including items that are already on sale, as well as a 10% savings on licensed fonts and ready-to-make projects from supported brands like Sanrio, Disney, Simplicity, and Anna Griffin.

Annual - $7.99 per month (billed once annually at $95.88)

With the monthly Cricut Access subscription, you are granted the unlimited use of over 400 fonts that are available in the Cricut Design Space, unlimited, unrestricted use of over 90,000 images that you can use for any design in the Cricut Design Space, 10% member savings on purchases from Cricut's website, including items that are already on sale, as well as a 10% savings on licensed fonts and ready-to-make projects from supported brands like Sanrio, Disney, Simplicity, and Anna Griffin. These are all available in the monthly tier of the subscription service, and they've added access to a Priority Member Care Line, which cuts wait times for customer support in half.

Premium - $9.99 per month (billed once annually at $119.88)

With the monthly Cricut Access subscription, you are granted the unlimited use of over 400 fonts that are available in the Cricut Design Space, unlimited, unrestricted use of over 90,000 images that you can use for any design in the Cricut Design Space, 10% member savings on purchases from Cricut's website, including items that are already on sale, as well as a 10% savings on licensed fonts and ready-to-make projects from supported brands like Sanrio, Disney, Simplicity, and Anna Griffin, as well as access to a Priority Member Care Line, which cuts wait times for customer support in half. These are available with your annual subscription. In addition to this, you get up to a 50% savings on licensed fonts, images, and ready-to-make projects, and free economy shipping on all orders from Cricut's website, over $50.

These member perks can be beneficial if you're going to be creating a lot of projects in a short amount of time. Again, it is in no way required for users to be Access members in order to take advantage of the Cricut Design Space or its user-friendly user interface, but these are the substantial rewards you can expect if you do sign up for membership!

Your First Design

The first thing that you'll get when you launch the Cricut Design Space for the first time, is a very quick tutorial on how to insert a shape, and how to fill that shape with a colored pattern. Go ahead and run through that process a few times until you're familiar with where the various assets and options are, so you can introduce a shape into the design Space, change the Linetype, and change what the shape is filled with. This will act as a head start for you in figuring out how to do more projects within the Cricut Design Space!

https://learn.cricut.com/design-space-for-beginners has a wealth of tutorial videos for various things you can do in the design space. Be sure to check there for tutorials, troubleshooting, and so much more.

Now that you've gotten a preliminary feel for some of the basics, let's run through a project and get you familiar with the entire process.

As the first step, we're going to select the "Text" option. In the text box that appears, we're going to type the phrase, "Good Vibes" and pick a font in the Design Space that you like. Do remember that some of the fonts in that list will have a cost. If you're looking for free fonts exclusively, you can choose the "System Fonts," which are the fonts that are already installed on your computer.

Once you've chosen a font that fits your vision for this project, ensure that the "Linetype" is set to "cut." Once you've made certain of this, you can click "Make it," in the upper right hand corner and follow the prompts. If your design looks right on the screen that pops up, you'll follow these next steps.

Using the measurements at the top of the Design Space, cut a piece of vinyl that is adequately-sized to accommodate your design. Get your light blue or light-grip Cricut Maker mat and line up your vinyl so your design will print on it. Make adjustments to where your design is in the Design Space if you need to!

Once you have your vinyl where you need it, use the rounded back of your scraper/burnishing tool to smooth the vinyl down on the gripped surface, working from the middle out toward the edges. Ensure that the piece is lying flat with no bubbles or wrinkles so you get the crispest and precise cuts possible.

Now that your vinyl is lined up on your mat, select the "vinyl" setting on your Cricut Explore model (skip this step if you have a Cricut Maker). Slide your mat under the white holding brackets in your Cricut maker. Once it's there, click "Continue" on the bottom right of the Cricut Design Space. The site will communicate with your machine and you'll be prompted to hit the double arrow button. This will lock the mat into place.

Once the Cricut C button is blinking, press it once and watch it work its magic! Once the machine has completed its cut, remove the mat from the machine and bring it to your crafting space. Using the rounded back of your scraper/burnishing tool, smooth the entire surface of the vinyl on your mat. This will help the carrier sheet hold onto the parts of your design that you don't want to weed.

Once you've thoroughly rubbed the entire piece, use your weeding tool to pick up the blanks around your letters. The background, the circles in your O and G, all the things you don't want to stick to your laptop. Once only the letters remain on the carrier sheet, cut an appropriately-sized piece of transfer tape. Using the back of your scraper, smooth the transfer tape down onto the entirety of your design. Once you've got a good grip on your design, peel the tape back from the carrier sheet.

Using some rubbing alcohol, clean the space on your laptop where you intend to place your design. Once it's completely clean, lay the design where you want it and rub it into place using the back of your scraper. Carefully peel back your transfer sheet to reveal your new design and admire your handiwork! You've just completed your first Cricut project! Look at you go!

Chapter 3: Your Cricut Materials

What Supplies Will I Need?

When you're starting to work on Cricut projects, there are some essentials that you will need in order to get started. Here is a breakdown of what those essentials are, if you're going to be doing a project on adhesive vinyl, as an example.

Your Cricut Machine

Once you pick the model that is best for you from the ones listed in the first chapter, you will want to have it set up, primed and ready, with the fine point blade loaded into accessory clamp B.

Cricut Machine Cutting Mat

This mat is a very simple, but integral part of the Cricut crafting process. Cricut has several thin mats, with an adhesive grip on them, as well as a grid. When your material is layered onto this mat and loaded into your Cricut machine, you can be sure your material will be right where it needs to be, in order to get the perfect cuts and strokes on it.

Because of its unique size and grip strength, this is one of the materials that is best left to the Cricut brand. Searching for another mat with equal abilities could end up being more costly, or just less effective.

Cricut brand is really the one to go with for this particular component.

Your Hand Tools

Some of the purposes fulfilled by the tools in this list can be fulfilled with items that you have around the house. However, Cricut does offer a starter kit that contains all these tools. This kit is very reasonably priced, and it contains everything you could need to get going.

The tools to look for when you're getting started are:

- **Weeding Tool** – This is a hook with a very fine point that allows you to peel blanks from your cut vinyl. This tool will come in handy for most, if not all the projects you do with your Cricut. It helps you to remove your design from the excess material without having to bend, fold, or fight with your material. This helps to keep the edges of your design crisp, clean and sharp every time.
- **Scraper/Burnishing Tool** – This simple tool will be your most-used Cricut tool, with the possible exception

of the weeding tool. You will find that once you lift your cut designs from the backing sheet, transferring them to your project surface will require even, steady pressure for burnishing your projects beautifully. This tool, in a pinch, can be replaced with other items, but this tool really does do the best work.

- **Scissors** – Any crafter knows that scissors are an integral part of their tool kit. While the scissors that Cricut offers are exceedingly sharp, with very fine points on each blade, any pair that is suited for your craft will serve you well here.

- **Craft Tweezers** – These reverse-action tweezers have a strong grip, precise points, and alleviate cramping after prolonged use. The ergonomic grip makes it possible to keep a tight grip on your materials throughout the project, giving you that extra set of hands you always wish you had while crafting.

- **Spatula** – Sometimes you feel like you need an extra set of hands when you're peeling or laying down a project. This tool gives you that extra support and maneuverability where you need it.

You'll find that these tools will help you to complete your first project, to a spectacular result each time you set out to use them.

Transfer Tape

Transfer tape is a clear, mild adhesive tape that comes in sheets. The purpose of this material is to take your freshly cut designs from their backing sheet, firmly hold them perfectly in place, which you may then burnish onto your project with ease. The adhesive is such that it won't damage your design or the material it's meant to go on.

Later in this book, you will find some tips on how to get the very most out of your transfer tape, each time you use it, and on choosing a transfer tape that you can get in a suitable grip strength, quality, and quantity that is most appropriate for your projects.

For instance, if you're doing a lot of projects on materials that have a very coarse or glittery surface, you will need a transfer tape with a higher grip strength to keep it in place while you're working on them.

Right out of the gate, I will tell you that the Cricut brand transfer tape comes in a single sheet that is rolled up, and which measures out to 12" x 48". You can cut the sheet to your liking, in any size or shape that is needed by your project, and each piece that you cut can be used multiple times before disposal.

These sheets from the Cricut brand are currently at $8.99 MSRP for your local crafting retailer, while some other brands offer a 6-10' roll of 12"-wide transfer tape for a comparable price.

For the best information on whose brands are best for the types of projects you like to do, YouTube is an invaluable resource that has information on the latest and greatest from the people who do these types of craft every day.

While transfer tape is an absolute necessity when doing projects with your Cricut machine, the brand is not nearly as important as having something to use. Do some shopping around, check out the tips in Chapter Six regarding transfer tape, find a sample size of the tapes you want to try, and get started!

Like with any new craft you're undertaking, it will wake a little bit of trial and error to find the supplies and products that best fir your needs, and which will work best for you in the long run.

Isopropyl or Rubbing Alcohol

Since adhesive is a main theme and part of the Cricut process, and the process of using your Cricut machine, it is imperative to make sure that the surfaces you're using (your mat, the materials, the item onto which your design will be burnished), should be cleansed of impurities as best as humanly possible.

Particularly with a slick surface like glass or ceramic, you will want to rub down the surface with some rubbing alcohol to remove any dirt, oil, debris, or anything that could compromise your design. If you wipe it down with rubbing alcohol, pat dry, then let stand for thirty seconds, your design will be ready to go!

Be certain that any paper towels or other products you're using for this step don't leave behind any fibers or debris that could compromise your design, particularly the smaller, or more intricate ones.

A Blank Stage for Your Design

This is the item onto which you'll be burnishing your design. It's important to know that while the world is your oyster and that there is very little unavailable to you with Cricut crafting, I recommend a flat surface for your first project. Being able to access the whole surface of this piece, without having to worry about curvature or other obstructions will make it much easier to learn how to work with your materials.

While a travel mug is a great idea for a Cricut project, doing it as your first might give you more trouble than you may have initially anticipated. We don't want you to start yourself out with a project that will give you trouble. Instead, consider putting a personalized design or phrase on your laptop, or on a binder.

A Computer with Internet Access

The Cricut Design Space can only be accessed with an active internet connection, so it's important to make sure your computer will have uninterrupted access throughout the course of your design!

You'll want to save your work often, just in case the connection hiccups. You wouldn't want to lose any design progress in such an event.

Self-Adhesive Vinyl

Last but not least, you will need a piece of self-adhesive vinyl that is your desired color and type. You'll be loading this onto your Cricut cutting mat, and your design will be cut out of it in no time at all!

That's all there is to it! With all these items, you're ready to tackles your first self-adhesive vinyl design!

What Materials Can I Use with My Cricut?

As you've likely read in this book already, Cricut boasts being able to work with more than 100 materials to make your projects come to life like never before. Thanks to the vast assortment of media that Cricut can bring to your crafting station, the sky is the limit for what you can do with your Cricut machine, no matter which model you've elected to purchase.

Here are 100 materials that your Cricut can use without issue!

Fabric
Polyester
Linen
Printable Fabric
Silk
Cotton Fabric
Wool Felt
Canvas
Metallic Leather
Oil Cloth
Felt
Faux Suede
Flannel
Denim
Burlap
Duck Cloth
Leather

Faux Leather
Foam
Glitter Foam
Craft Foam
Foil
Aluminum Foil
Embossable
Foil
Aluminum
Sheets
Foil Poster
Board
Foil Embossed
Paper
Adhesive Foil
Foil Iron-On
Foil Acetate

Paper
Poster Board
Contact Paper
Metallic Paper
Glitter
Cardstock
Solid Core
Cardstock
Flocked
Cardstock
Printable
Sticker Paper
Notebook Paper
Parchment
Paper
Photo Framing
Mat

Metallic Vellum
Vellum
Freezer Paper
Metallic Cardstock
Flocked Paper
Metallic Poster Board
Corrugated Paper
Peal Cardstock
Glitter Paper
Paper Board
Tissue Paper
Rice Paper
Cardboard
Shimmer Paper
Pearl Paper
Craft Paper
Photographs
Cardstock
Temporary Tattoo Paper
Copy Paper
Washi Sheets
Scrapbook Paper
Post Its

Construction Paper
Washi Tape
Paper Grocery Bags
Adhesive Cardstock
Wrapping Paper

Plastic
Shrink Plastic
Transparency Film
Duct Tape
Window Cling
Magnet Sheets
Plastic Packaging
Stencil Material
Printable Magnet Sheets

Vinyl
Holographic Iron-On
Removable Adhesive Vinyl
Flocked Iron-On
Neon Iron-On
Matte Vinyl

Metallic Vinyl
Stencil Vinyl
Outdoor Vinyl
Adhesive Vinyl
Printable Vinyl
Printable Iron-On
Glitter Vinyl
Glossy Vinyl
Glossy Iron-On
Chalkboard Vinyl
Matte Iron-On
Glitter Iron-On
Permanent Adhesive Vinyl
Dry Erase Vinyl
Holographic Vinyl
Metallic Iron-On
Paint Chips

Wood
Chipboard
Wood Veneer
Adhesive Wood
Corkboard
Balsa Wood
Birch Wood

What Can My Cricut Do?

There really isn't any limit to how much you can do with your Cricut machine. However, if you're short on ideas, here are some that I've thrown together to get your creative juices flowing!

Take a look through this list and come up with some things that you think would fit well with the types of designs that you like to make!

Make felt dolls
Beautifully address envelopes
Create doll clothing
Make greeting cards of every design and style
Create placards
Cut items out of balsa wood
Cut washi tape shapes
Craft borders and decorations for your corkboard
Dream up refrigerator magnets

Customize wedding invitations
Create holiday crafts
Design or decorate purses and wallets
Cut your own craft foam shapes
Create decals and patterns for pillows and cushions
Create your own coloring book pages
Cut fabric with precision
Make jewelry
Make party favors

Create 3D bouquets
Cut leather
Cut your own party hats
Make themed window clings
Create fabric appliques
Create temporary tattoos
Create glassware decals
Design personalized gift tags
Create clothes for your pet
Create custom gift boxes

Customize baby clothes
Design creative pin cushions
Create cake toppers
Customize holiday ornaments
Custom Coasters
Create sewing patterns
Create themed t-shirt transfers
Make personalized fabric key fobs
Cut perfect quilting squares
Create and embellish your own holiday stockings
Craft decorations to fit any theme
Design dust covers
Cut unique stencils
Create stickers & decals
Design door Hangers
Create jigsaw puzzles
Add pizzazz to headbands
Create fabric accessories and embellishments
Cut patterns to make your own socks and embellishments
Create wedding place cards
Make 3D papercraft shapes
Write beautiful signs in calligraphy
Create cupcake flags
Craft cushion transfers
Design 3D and flat-panel wall art of any theme
Cut scrapbook embellishments

Chapter 4: Cricut Projects for Beginners

Technique

By far the best technique I can teach you, which will help you get closer to pulling off the perfect project is patience. Take the time to relax, take your time in getting the material to do what you want it to do, and think of creative solutions. Doing so will always yield a greater rate of success with your projects made with the Cricut system. Always go into your projects with a positive attitude that says, "I can do this!" In addition to this, bring a quizzical mindset that asks, "How can I do this differently?" With those and a lot of patience, you will find that your projects roll by quickly and much more smoothly. Plus, you'll have so much more fun when you do it this way!

In the sections below, you will find more specifics on ways in which to boost the quality of the crafts you create, and ways to work that make things go more smoothly! We have a lot of information to cover on the subjects of extending the life of your accessories and materials, as well as ways to use them as economically as possible!

Let's Get Down to It!

Immediately out of the box, you'll find that your Cricut Explore machine will come with some cardstock, a pen, a blade and a mat. These tools will get you through the very first of your beginner's projects.

As you get the hang of using the Cricut Design Space application and how the Cricut machine operates, you will find that your skill level with the Cricut system will increase rather rapidly. These beginner projects are all just the right skill level for someone who's starting out with their Cricut machine, so pick the one you like and get to work!

Cricut Hello Greeting Card

Take the protective plastic layer off the top of your green Cricut cutting mat and set it aside. Be sure to keep it somewhere it won't become wrinkled or damaged, as this is the layer you'll put back on top of your mats before each time you store them. This will protect its adhesive finish, giving your mats more lasting power throughout your projects.

Line up your cardstock with the upper left-hand corner of the grip on your mat, keeping the textured side of the cardstock facing upward. Smooth down your cardstock with your hands to ensure that no gaps, wrinkles, or folds form in your cardstock.

Once you've lines up your cardstock with the corner of your mat, place the mat under the mat guides in your Cricut machine. Firmly push the mat toward the rollers as you tap the Load/Unload button, which is indicated by the double arrow, on the top of your machine.

Open accessory clamp A inside your machine and remove the cap from your metallic Cricut pen, which came with your machine. Place the cap on the back of your pen and slide it snugly into place so you don't lose it while you're working. Once you've done that, gently push up on the bottom of accessory clamp A while you insert the pen. Push gently but firmly into the clamp until the little arrow on the pen is covered by the clamp and you hear a click. Close the clamp and remove your finger from underneath it.

Now that your machine is loaded and set up with the correct accessories, you will find that you're ready to start your design. If you're having trouble finding the project, or if Cricut Design Space doesn't automatically prompt you to begin with this design, click on the menu and select New Machine Setup. Follow the initial steps once more until the application pulls up the project for you. Alternatively, you can use the project search function with the keyword "Phone." This should pull up the two-layered greeting card design that we're creating here.

Click the "Make It" button to ensure that the design is correctly lined up with the materials on your mat. If this screen is showing you that your design will be cut in a space that isn't covered by your cardstock, unload the mat, adjust your cardstock, then reload it and return to the "Make It" screen, or return to the design space and adjust where the design is laid out. Once everything is plotted out properly, return the mat to the machine, and return to the "Make It" screen.

Set the dial on the outside of your Cricut Explore machine to the "cardstock" setting to ensure that your machine will be applying the appropriate amount of pressure to your blade. This will give you the cleanest, most accurate cuts possible.

Once everything appears to be in order, click the "Go" option. On your Cricut machine, once the Cricut C button begins to blink, give it a press. Your machine will set itself to the task of drawing and cutting your design!

Once that's complete, tap the blinking Load/Unload button and remove your mat from the Cricut machine. Open accessory clamp A, remove your pen, and replace the cap to ensure your pen won't dry out while you're working. Once your pen is capped, put it in the storage compartment in the front of your machine. Now you will always know where it is!

To release your work from the mat, flip it face down on your work surface, so the back of the mat is facing you. Gently curl the corner of your mat back toward you until the cardstock releases from the adhesive surface of your mat. Using your free hand, hold the cardstock down onto your work surface, applying pressure evenly to keep your project from curling as you release it from the mat.

Fold the cardstock in half evenly, then repeat this step with the blue paper that came with your machine. Once they're both folded evenly, place the paper inside the card so it shows through the cut spaces in your cardstock.

Congratulations on completing your very first Cricut Design Project! You're doing great.

Happy Birthday Gift Tag

Special materials for this project include three different colors of cardstock to your preference, a roll-on adhesive tape, and a glue pen. If you find that other types of adhesive would work better for you, feel free to use those instead.

Visit the Cricut Design Space web application and select the option to create a new project. Once you're there, click

"Images," and search for the word "tag." Select the shape that looks a plain gift tag like this: Once you've selected this image, you should see populate in the queue at the bottom of your screen.

Now, click the "Categories" option at the top of the screen and select the "Birthday" category, before setting your search filter to "Phrases." Select the Happy Birthday to You image of your choice by clicking on it. We chose the one that looks like it's on a wavy banner.

Once you've made your selection for both images, you can click the green "Insert Images," button in the bottom corner of your screen. This will add the images to your design space so you can manipulate them to fit the design you'd like to create.

Drag the tag image closer to upper left-hand corner of the Cricut Design Space and use the arrow button on the bottom right of the image so you can resize it to the desired dimensions.

The next thing you'll want to do is use the circular arrow button to rotate the tag 90° so your Happy Birthday image will fit onto the tag with some simple resizing. When you drag the phrase over to your tag however, you may notice that the text disappears beneath the tag image. This is not a problem, as you can simply click "Arrange" at the top of your screen and select the "Move to Front," option. This will put the phrase over the gift tag so it's plainly visible.

Now, let's resize that phrase so it fits properly on the tag with no issues. Click the arrow in the bottom right corner and drag it until the design is properly sized for your project.

Now, let's address the color of your images. While the Cricut machine does not print or affect the color of the materials you're using, it does differentiate where to make its cuts based on the color of the materials in its dock. In order to keep your own thinking straight on what cardstock to put where, and to keep your Cricut cutting properly, set your images in Cricut Design Space to fit the color of the cardstock you have on hand.

On the right side of your screen, you'll se a panel that shows you each layer of your design. Simply click on the layer of the image you wish to change; color options will pop up next to the panel. From here, you can simply select the color that most closely fits the cardstock you've chosen for this portion of your project.

If two layers of your project should be the same color, you can make things a little easier in the cutting process by consolidating both of those elements of your design onto the same layer. Simply drag one layer of your design to the one with which you wish to pair it and drop. This will put them both together and will keep them the same color!

Once you've gotten all the elements of your project to look the way you want, click "Save," give your project a unique name that you'll remember and click "Save," again. Next, you'll click "Make It," to start the cutting process.

The mat preview screen will show you every step of the cutting process and where on your materials the cuts will be made. Each of these elements will be separated by color, so you can tell what cuts will be made on your different pieces of cardstock.

If you're interested in making multiple gift tags, simply change the Project Copies quantity to your preferred number, then click "Apply." This will update your view to show you where the cuts will be made on the various colors of cardstock that you've selected.

Images in the preview screen cannot be manipulated in any way, so if you still have changes to make at this stage of the process, simply go back to the Design space, make your changes there so the project is laid out to your specifications, then return to the "Make It" screen to reassess and to start the cutting process.

Once everything looks like it's laid out the way you need it, click the "Continue" button. You will be prompted to take the next steps of your project.

At this stage of the process, you will want to ensure that the material dial on the outside of your Cricut Explore machine is set to "Cardstock," so all the cuts are made as precisely as possible.

Take the first cardstock that is shown on the prompt screen and line it up on your mat. Be sure to line the material up so it's square with the grid and the grip on the mat. It will line up with the corners of the grid when done properly. Smooth the material down with your hands, making sure no noticeable gaps, wrinkles, or folds form on the material.

Place the mat into the machine by sliding it under the mat guides. Keep the mat pressed firmly to the rollers before tapping the Load/Unload button. Once the Cricut C button begins to blink, tap it and watch your machine spring into action.

To release your work from the mat, flip it face down on your work surface, so the back of the mat is facing you. Gently curl the corner of your mat back toward you until the cardstock releases from the adhesive surface of your mat. Using your free hand, hold the cardstock down onto your work surface, applying pressure evenly to keep your project from curling as you release it from the mat.

Once you've done this step, you'll find that all that's left on the mat are your design pieces, and some blanks in the lettering. Use your weeding tool to remove the blanks, and the spatula to remove your design pieces from the mat.

Use your Scraper/Burnishing Tool to remove any remaining blanks or cut cardstock on your mat.

Once your mat is clear, load the next piece of cardstock, as indicated by the screen on Cricut Design Space.

Place the mat into the machine by sliding it under the mat guides. Keep the mat pressed firmly to the rollers before tapping the Load/Unload button.

Once the Cricut C button begins to blink, tap it and watch your machine spring into action.

To release your work from the mat, flip it face down on your work surface, so the back of the mat is facing you. Gently curl the corner of your mat back toward you until the cardstock releases from the adhesive surface of your mat. Using your free hand, hold the cardstock down onto your work surface, applying pressure evenly to keep your project from curling as you release it from the mat.

Once you've done this step, you'll find that all that's left on the mat are your design pieces, and some blanks in the lettering. Use your weeding tool to remove the blanks, and the spatula to remove your design pieces from the mat.

Use your Scraper/Burnishing Tool to remove any remaining blanks or cut cardstock on your mat.

Once your mat is clear, load the last piece of cardstock, as indicated by the screen on Cricut Design Space.

Place the mat into the machine by sliding it under the mat guides. Keep the mat pressed firmly to the rollers before tapping the Load/Unload button.

Once the Cricut C button begins to blink, tap it and watch your machine spring into action.

To release your work from the mat, flip it face down on your work surface, so the back of the mat is facing you. Gently curl the corner of your mat back toward you until the cardstock releases from the adhesive surface of your mat. Using your free hand, hold the cardstock down onto your work surface, applying pressure evenly to keep your project from curling as you release it from the mat.

Once you've done this step, you'll find that all that's left on the mat are your design pieces, and some blanks in the lettering. Use your weeding tool to remove the blanks, and the spatula to remove your design pieces from the mat.

Use your Scraper/Burnishing Tool to remove any remaining blanks or cut cardstock on your mat. Be sure to return the protective cover to your mat before storing it.

Once all your pieces have been cut, click Finish on the Design Space browser window.

When assembling your project, it will be easiest to work from the bottom layer, working up to the top layer. Keep the Cricut Design Space open to your project so you can reference it as you put it together.

Using your roll-on adhesive tape—or your preferred means of adhesive—secure the bottom later to the next layer.

Using a glue pen—or your preferred means of adhesive—secure the details to your lettering layer. Once that's completed, mount the lettering onto your tag, and you're all finished!

That's a gift that keeps on giving.

Wooden Welcome Sign with Vinyl Designs

For this project, you will need self-adhesive vinyl, transfer tape, a weeding tool, a knife that is either the TrueControl or another precision blade, your scraper or burnishing tool, a trimmer or scissors, and a wood plaque that is painted or stained to your preference.

Open your browser and navigate to the Cricut Design Space. Logging in will be your first step, if you're not already logged in. This will give you access to all your assets, designs, and elements. Once you're logged in, click "New Project."

Select the "Text" option on the left-hand side. Once the text box pops up onto your screen, type WELCOME into the dialog box alongside the text box. Once you've typed that, you will see the text box populate with the same text.

Now, it's time to choose the font that best fits this project. Pick one that is to your liking. A simple, sans serif font is recommended this project. Be sure to pay mind to whether or not the font you've chosen is paid.

Add any additional text you would like on your welcome plaque in a new line under your WELCOME. Your family name, or maybe a fun slogan is recommended for this playful, decorative project. Once you've chosen that, resize it to the same width of your welcome. Both lines of text should be just slightly narrower than the width of your wood plaque.

Put both of your text boxes onto the same layer, picking the one with the weight that works best for your project.

Put some distance between the text boxes to leave enough room for a large monogram. This image will go in between the lines of text.

Click "Images" and set your filter for Single Layer Images, then search for keyword "monogram." Select one that you like and click "Insert Images."

Place your monogram in between your layers of text and resize it until it all comes together.

For some added flair, let's curve the WELCOME text. Using a blank shape as a guide for this curve can help us line up our letters evenly. Select the "Circle" shape, stretch it into an oval that has the desired curve, and place it over your monogram, beneath your WELCOME.

Now that we've placed that guide, which we will be removing once we're finished lining up our letters, it's time to separate the letters in our WELCOME so we can place them individually along that curve.

With the text selected, click the "Advanced" tab at the top of the screen, then click "Ungroup To Letters." This will now allow you to place each letter individually along that curve. Be sure to adjust the rotation of your letters, so the whole word is placed on that curve.

Delete your placeholder oval.

Review your text and image and make any last-minute changes you may need to make so your design is completely to your liking.

Once everything is in order, click Select All in the top menu, then click "Attach" at the bottom right-hand corner of your screen. The attach option will have a little paperclip icon beneath it.

Once that's done, you will notice all layers are combined into one. Edit the color of your—now single—image to match your material.

Click "Save," name your project, then click "Save" again.

Click "Make It" to start the cutting process. This will show you where your cuts will appear on the material on your mat.

Set the dial on your machine to vinyl. Line your vinyl up with the upper left-hand corner of the grip on your mat, ensuring that the backing of your vinyl is face down. Smooth down your vinyl with your hands so no gaps, wrinkles, or folds form in your vinyl.

Once you have that lined up on your mat, place the mat under the guides in your Cricut machine. Gently push the mat toward the rollers as you hit the Load/Unload button (indicated by the double arrow) on the top of your machine.

Press the blinking Cricut C button and watch your project come to life.

Once the material is fully cut, press the Load/Unload button to release your mat from the machine. Using a precision blade, make an L shaped cut around your design to release most of the excess vinyl from the mat. Roll up the excess and save it for later use.

Using your scraper tool, burnish the design before weeding. This will help the elements of your design stay stuck to the carrier sheet while you weed!

Now, holding the weeding tool at a slight angle, hook onto the blank vinyl around your design and gently pull up the pieces you don't need. You can collect them in a bin to the side or in the trash. Once you've removed all the small negative pieces of vinyl, you can remove the larger sheet of vinyl around your design.

Grasp the vinyl in the upper left-hand corner, pulling back gently and slowly continue to pull down diagonally toward the lower right-hand corner. Watch for any pieces of your design that stick to the blank vinyl you're removing. Using the back of your weeding hook, you can gently guide those pieces of your design back down onto the carrier sheet.

Once all that's left on your carrier sheet at the elements of your design, it's time to cut the transfer tape! Carefully place the transfer tape over your entire design. Do your best to avoid bubbles, but a couple here and there won't do you any harm!

Use your scraper tool to thoroughly burnish your design into the transfer tape, then peel the carrier sheet away from the transfer tape. This will leave your design stuck to the transfer tape, with the adhesive side of your vinyl exposed.

Gently place your vinyl design onto your plaque, making sure to center it completely before allowing the adhesive to touch the surface of your plaque. Once you have it lined up exactly where you want it, use your scraper to burnish your design onto the surface of your plaque.

Now, carefully peel the transfer tape from the upper left-hand corner down diagonally, toward the lower right-hand corner. If any pieces of your design try to come with your transfer tape, simply lay it back down, burnish again, then resume peeling.

Your vinyl creation should now be proudly displayed on the front of your wooden plaque!

Chapter 5: Cricut Projects for Skilled Users

As you begin to get into the types of projects that require more skill, you will find that you will need to branch out to websites that offer their own design and cut files that you can use to make more and more creative things.

Because of this, I would recommend looking to various online resources for projects you can do to broaden your horizons when it comes to more complex projects!

To give you some ideas to get you started on where to look, here is a list of 100 crafts you can do with your Cricut system to truly make your crafts unique to you!

3D Wood Puzzles

You may have seen these in museum gift shops or in the section of the toy store for the brainy kids. These are amazing fun and they make such a great final product when put together.

3D Foam Puzzles

Foam is just as sturdy for 3D puzzles, and you can take them apart, put them back together, knock them down, and more and they bounce right back. These make such a great gift for young children.

3D Wall Art

Art that pops off your wall and makes a statement about who you are to all your guests is something people pay a lot of money to have. Put a little piece of your creative self on your wall and show off your creativity!

Aprons

If you have a lot of passion in the kitchen, your apron is a great way to add a personalized touch to your experience. With a character you love, a funny saying, or just a monogram, you can totally own the kitchen.

Banners

Any occasion is made more official with a banner! With Cricut, you can use your materials to make a banner that is unique, and which will beautifully commemorate the occasion at hand.

Beanies

For any outdoor activity that's going to be happening during the winter months, a knit cap is a great way to keep warm. Having one with your own design emblazoned on the side is sure to not only elevate the style of the hat, but to make others wonder where they can get one just like it!

Beer Steins

The dollar store will often have blank glass beer mugs that are basically calling out to crafters to decorate them. Make a memorable gift for the beer lover in your life!

Bookmarks

Bookmarks are such a simple craft, but they're almost always needed! If your circle is like mine, everyone around you is in the middle of reading a book at all times. Replace the grocery receipt in the middle of their book with something fun and personal!

Bumper Stickers

Something to occupy the drivers behind you in traffic will always be in style. Make some fun statements for you and your friends to put on the bumper!

Business Cards

Business cards that are cut from premium stock and in unique shapes can be *so* expensive. Printing your designs on cardstock with a standard printer and cutting out dynamic designs is sure to catch the eye of potential customers.

Business Marketing Materials

Why stop at business cards when you can make standees, door hangers, and so much more?

Cake Toppers

Got a themed birthday party coming up? Use plastic or metal to make a beautifully themed cake topper that will blow away your guests!

Calendars

No matter how the times progress, you always need to know what day it is! See what unique calendars you can make for your desk or office!

Candles

Sure, you can't make candles themselves with your Cricut. But you could get a candle in a blank glass holder and put something PERFECT for any occasion on the outside of it. These make ideal gifts, let me tell you.

Canvas Tote Bags

Tote bags are one of the most useful accessories on the planet. Keep all your things together and add some style with your Cricut! Heck, if you felt like it, you could get some canvas and *make your own tote bag*!

Car Decals

Got a business? Tell the world about it as you travel through your week!

Centerpieces

Any large-scale event could benefit from themed centerpieces to amuse and wow your guests!

Clothing

Put your creative flourish on anything you own with Cricut and the numerous materials they have to offer. Whether it's an iron-on decal or a fabric embellishment, there's no shortage of ways to impress!

Coasters

Like so many other things in this list, coasters can make such a great gift for housewarming or holidays. Everyone could use a unique set of coasters to keep their surfaces safe and dry!

Coffee Mugs

Coffee mugs are probably the one dish in my house that I will always want more of when I see them. They're great for so many things and having ones that are uniquely you are the perfect addition to any office or kitchen.

Coloring Pages

Using the pen in your Cricut, you can download line art to make coloring pages of any style or theme for yourself or your loved ones! If you have children in your family coming to visit, this makes for a great group activity!

Commemorative Plates

Did you know that come Cricut materials that can adhere to ceramic could make a great embellishment for decorative of commemorative plates? What occasions could you commemorate?

Craft Foam Shape Sets

Just like with the puzzle sets, you can cut just about any shape you want out of craft foam. Doing so on the foam sheets with an adhesive backing could allow you to make your own little crafting sets of any theme you desire! This includes letters as well!

Decorative Plaques

Just as you saw in the Cricut Projects for Beginners section, decorative plaques are a breeze and, as you gain more competence with the Cricut system, you can get more intricate and creative!

DIY Craft Kits

Making crafting kit components with the Cricut is a breeze. Let your imagination run wild on what pieces you could bundle together for someone to make their own crafting projects! Let your mind run wild on this one as they make wonderful party favors, gifts for children or crafters, and so much more!

DIY Decals

The decals you create can be placed onto a carrier or backing sheet to be given out. If you don't want to put your decal right onto something, simply top with a piece of transfer tape and give away!

Doilies

The intricate designs that Cricut can do allows you to make doilies of *so* many different materials, colors, sizes, shapes, themes and more!

Envelopes

Did you know that envelopes are made out of one continuous piece of paper that is just cut, folded, and glued in a specific way? This means that you can take any piece of paper you like, with any print you like, and make an envelope out of it! Go nuts!

Flowerpots

A flowerpot can be sort of a mundane piece. However, with some craft paint and a stencil that you made with your Cricut, or with a decal, they can transform into something that fits your décor perfectly!

Framed Affirmations

This life is tough! Affirmations that you can put in your own font or style can make all the difference in the vibe you get from a personal space. Jazz up your own and put them all over your space!

Gift Card Envelopes

These can be done with scrapbooking paper, construction paper, foil paper, or anything, really. You can elevate this tiny little gift into something truly personal that anyone would love to have.

Gift Tags

As you saw in the Cricut Projects for Beginners section, these tags can take any simple gift and give it such a creative pop. Going that little extra bit toward making someone's gift look and feel unique really does make a difference.

Greeting Cards

Some of the most gorgeous greeting cards at the supermarket these days can run you about $9 per card! With the materials to hand in your crafting station, you can make cards that are just gorgeous, multi-layered, and make them carry your personal message. It makes the whole gift so much more personal and meaningful.

Hats

There are patterns to make your own hats, as well as decals you can make that will make an existing hat pop!

Holiday Décor

I can't even be honest with you about how nuts I've gone in this category. There are so many decorations you can make for any and every occasion that you just can't even imagine doing all of them for every holiday!

Hoodies

Nothing is more comforting than a nice thick hoodie, sometimes. Put your own personal touch on a hoodie or carry around the mark of your favorite characters or phrases.

Jewelry

Oh yes. You can absolutely make your own jewelry with the materials available through Cricut. Leather, fabric, metal... It's all there.

Keepsake Boxes

No craft is complete if it can't, in some way, be tied back to keepsake boxes, right? They're all over the crafting world and you can absolutely make keepsake boxes or just decorate them to the nines!

Key Fobs

Make your keys stand out by making an adorable or stylish fey fob!

Keychains

Got a favorite character or emoji? Make a keychain!

Labeled Kitchenware

From canisters to kitchen crocks, there's nothing you can't decal!

Labels

If organization is your forte, using Cricut can help you make gorgeous labels for every room of the house!

Lanyards

Keep your keys or ID cards displayed with style and comfort.

Leather Accents

From scrapbooking to home décor, leather accents can really elevate your designs from looking great, to looking completely professional.

Leather Accessories

Wrist bands, wallets, lanyards, money clips and more. Your Cricut can transform sheets of leather into your most gorgeous, stylish accessories.

Luggage Tags

Never be unsure of which bag on the carousel is you. Make a luggage tag that stands apart from the crowd as much as you do and claim your bag in no time!

Magnetic Poetry Sets

By printing words onto a set of printable magnets, you can create a set to make magnetic poems and limericks on your doors, refrigerators, or metal tables!

Magnetic Puzzles

Puzzles are a timeless gift that are always fun. Print a picture of a loved one onto a printable magnet, make a jigsaw puzzle and create a beautiful set for the front of your refrigerator, or for a friend!

Magnetic Storytelling Sets

By printing words onto a set of printable magnets, you can create a set to make magnetic stories and jokes on your doors, refrigerators, or metal tables!

Magnets

Think outside the box and make magnetic designs to your own liking and cut them into unique shapes to put your own style on your refrigerator or door!

Make Up Bags

Personalizing a simple zippered bag can make all the difference in the style of that item! Make it yours! You could even make your own zippered bag with your Cricut, and then decorate it!

Mandala Decals

Mandalas are gorgeous and Cricut is the perfect tool to help you to make decals to put on just about anything.

Mason Jars

Mason jars are good for everything from drinking to decoration, so the sky is the limit with this one! See what unique things you can put on yours.

Monogram Decals

Make everything so very uniquely you with monograms on all your accessories.

Name Plates

Crafter in Chief. Caren Smith, Crafter Extraordinaire. HBIC. The Big Cheese. Whatever you want people to see on your desk or office, you can make it happen!

Onesies

Blank onesies are about three dollars on their own. With one of these and the perfect iron-on decal, you can make a baby shower gift that every new mom will cherish.

Origami

Did you know that the scoring stylus makes *perfect* folding lines? Use your Cricut to cut and score an origami template and go nuts!

Oven Mitts

Oven mitts and potholders have a perfect place on the back of them for iron-on decals that show your personality. Between these and your apron, all your guests will hail to the chef.

Party Hats

These are so much easier than you think, seriously. Give it a look and put together the design of your dreams. It's so easy.

Party Invitations

Who's coming to your party? Everyone, because your invitations were *gorgeous* and now everyone is excited. Slam dunk.

Pennant Banners

These are so simple and cute, they're perfect or just about any party. Use twine to string them together and you have a beautiful rustic aesthetic.

Pennants

Support your kids at little league or make them for your next touch football game! Pennants are a really fun and simple decoration.

Personalized Clipboards

If you're an organization fanatic like myself, clipboards are pretty special objects and having one that says the right things on the back just seals the deal.

Photo Magnets

Magnets that have printed photos on them really does just bring a little part of the family love to the kitchen. You can also use these to print images of characters and slogans that you love!

Pillow Shams

Create or decorate pillow shams for your guest room to really make your guests feel at home!

Pillowcases

Cases for your throw pillows or bedroom pillows. Need I say more?

Pin Cushions

With all the fabric cutting capabilities that Cricut has, you can make an astounding number of things including a pin cushion that looks like just about anything you could ever want.

Pins

Show your love and support with statement buttons!

Place Cards

Effortless and gorgeous place cards with Cricut. Knock out 100 in no time at all and add that extra flair to any event.

Purses

Create, decorate, elevate, whichever you prefer!

Puzzles

Decoupage any image onto some chipboard and you are on your way to making a perfect little jigsaw puzzle! These make amazing personal gifts.

Quilled Designs

Paper quilling is a huge craft. Cut perfectly symmetrical strips of paper for your quilling and get rolling!

Quilting Squares

Quilting is a craft that has so many steps. Make one of those steps so much easier by cutting perfectly symmetrical squares every single time with ease.

Quilts

Why stop at squares? Sew those suckers together for yourself and make a beautiful blanket for you and your family to enjoy!

Recipe Card Dividers

I can't find the recipe card dividers that perfectly fit my style. I'll make them!

Return Address Labels

Sticker paper is easy to come by. Make your own beautiful return address labels!

Save the Date Cards

Printed items are such a large part of any wedding budget. Hack that budget down and DIY!

Sealing Stickers

Elevate your letters and other mail with a beautiful sticker that tells everyone the letter is from you with love.

Sewing Patterns

If sewing is your thing, you can get patterns for just about any design, cut them out, and get moving! Make your wardrobe completely uniquely you!

Shot Glasses

Great gifts as well as great for your kitchen. Blank shot glasses are so reasonably priced, and you can make them with your own flair!

Stationery

Making your own personalized letter writing materials gives it that extra personal touch without the prohibitive cost.

Stencils

Imagine seeing a design you love online, cutting out your own stencil, and putting that design into your own home. It's *that* easy.

Stickers

Stickers are great for so many different things. Marking dates in your calendar or planner, gifts for kids, reminders, decorating your envelopes, decorating memos, giving feedback on schoolwork, and so much more.

Tea Towels

Tea towels have an infinite number of uses in the kitchen and they're classically very well designed. Add your own flair to some towels!

Teacups

Teacups are like coffee mugs. You just cannot have too many of them and personalizing them is so easy. Go nuts!

Travel Mugs

Okay, so coffee mugs, but *to go*. So, these are even better than coffee mugs, of which you can never have too many, so please go nuts with these as well.

Trivets

Making trivets can be as simple as buying a single ceramic tile, putting your design onto it, and giving it a clear coat. Bam, a personalized trivet that will save your table from scorching under the hottest dishes.

T-Shirts

No group activity is quite the same without a commemorative t-shirt, right? Wow your friends and make them swag they'll never want to lose!

Tumblers

Another drinking vessel to bear your creative mark!

Wall Clings

Affirmations, designs, icons, labels, anything you want to put up on your wall for décor and for your family.

Wall Décor

Little signs that fit your décor theme, chalkboards, placards, and so much more can be created with the Cricut system.

Wallets

Leather, paper, felt, whatever fabric you want to use to make your wallets is up to you!

Water Bottles

Stay hydrated while sporting your personal style along the way!

Wedding Invitations

Every couple is looking for the invites that fit their theme and budget. This is the answer!

Wedding Party Gifts

From personalized emergency kits, to wine glasses, to hats, to beer cozies. You can make just about any gift for your wedding party with the help of your Cricut.

Wedding Table Numbers

No matter the size of the style, the Cricut can help you to make any shape or style to fit your theme!

Window Clings

Celebrate the holiday, occasion, or even just your favorite things with window clings to put around the home, office, or car!

Wine Glasses

Bottoms up! Whatever sentiments you'd like to immortalize on your favorite glasses is perfect for this.

Wood Décor

With the rustic aesthetic being as popular as it is these days, wood décor is coming back in such a big way. Get out there and make some of the cutest wooden accents for your home and then invite everyone over to show them off!

Wooden Snowflake Ornaments

A winter woodland theme is so perfect for the holidays. Aside from this, having flat, wood ornaments that are easy to store without breaking is every homeowner's dream!

There is *nothing* you can't do with Cricut!

Chapter 6: FAQs, Troubleshooting, & Cricut Hacks

Frequently Asked Questions

This section will address the most commonly asked questions about the Cricut experience, as well as some of the most common issue that come up throughout the process. If there is an answer that you need, which you cannot find here, you will find the internet to be an exceptionally useful tool in answering nearly any questions, troubleshooting mostly any issue, and just getting a better understanding of your Cricut system.

Why can't I weed my design without it tearing?

There are two fairly common causes for this type of issue. Number one is dull blades. We have some tips on how to sharpen your blades later in this section, so just look for that! The second reason is a build up of residues on your blades. Look further into this section for tips on how to clean your blades as well!

Is it necessary to turn all my images into SVGs?

No, it is not necessary to convert your images to the SVG format if you have a JPG or PNG. However, if it is your wish to have

SVG files in your project, there are several free online resources that can help you with this process. Try to keep in mind that if you convert your file type to an SVG, you may have less freedom to manipulate the components of your image.

Where do I go to buy materials?

When it comes to buying materials for your Cricut, there are nearly an unlimited number of places where you can get them. Since the Cricut is such a versatile machine with the ability to cut so many materials, you won't be able to go into any crafting or fabric stores without tripping over new materials you can use for your latest and greatest crafts.

As you continue to learn more about how Cricut works and what you can do with it, you will find which materials and brands best suit your needs. From there, you will often find what you need by shopping online to get the best prices and quantities of the materials you prefer, which will help you stretch your dollar as best as you can.

Do I need a printer to use my Cricut?

In a word, no. Using your Cricut with the materials we've laid out in this book doesn't require ink from a printer, though there are some materials on the market for Cricut, which are specifically meant to be printed on before using.

If you're not using these items, then you will find that you can get the most out of your machine without that feature.

If you wish to print things, then cut them, this is known as the Print then Cut method and there is a wealth of knowledge about this on the internet. You can make iron-on decals, tattoos, and so much more!

Where can I get images to use with my Cricut?

The beautiful thing about the Cricut Design Space and its ability to host so many different file types, is that you can upload images from any source, so long as you have the legal rights to use that image. Pulling images off of Google Image Search is done amongst crafters, but if you're selling the design in any way, you will want to make sure that the images you're using are either open license, or you've purchased them for use and distribution.

Do I have to buy all my fonts through Cricut?

Cricut Design Space has an option when looking through your fonts to use fonts that are installed on your computer. This is called "System Fonts." Ant font you can buy, or download can be used through Cricut Design Space with little to no issues. There are many resources for this on the internet as well.

However, if there is a font you're using, do make sure that you have the license to use the font for the purposes you have in mind for that font! Fonts, just like pictures, do have copyrights and can be limited in what they allow you to do with them.

Why is my blade cutting through my backing sheet?

This can be due to improper seating on the blade in the housing, so just pop the housing out, re-seat the blade inside, reload, and try again. This can *also* be due to an improper setting on the material dial. If you're cutting something very thin, but have the dial set to cardstock, your needle could be plunging right through the whole piece of material and its backing!

Why aren't my images showing up right on my mat?

It is possible, when you click "Make It," that the print preview of your project doesn't look anything like how you have it laid out in Design Space. If this is the case, go back to Design Space, highlight all your images, click "Group," then click "Attach." This should keep everything right where it needs to be for all your project cutting needs!

I'm just getting started, do I need to buy all of Cricut's accessories right away?

No, you won't need all the accessories right at once, and some of them you won't ever need at all, depending on what crafts you intend to do with your Cricut machine. In fact, you can use crafting items you likely already have on hand to get started, buying tools and accessories here and there as you get more use out of your machine! It is, by no means, necessary to spend a small fortune on accessories and tools just to do your first Cricut crafting project!

Which Cricut machines at compatible with design space?

The Cricut models that are currently compatible are all of the motorized cutting machines they have on the market! This means the Cricut Explore, Cricut Explore Air, Cricut Explore Air 2, and the Cricut Maker. You can use all these tools with the current version of Design Space to create countless projects for every style and occasion. Outdated machinery will need to be tested with the application to see if they're compatible, as Cricut does provide regular updates for the application that could nullify that compatibility over time.

Do I need to be connected to the internet to use design space?

Cricut Design Space is a web-based application that utilizes the cloud. Because of this, you do need an active, high-speed internet connection in order to make use of the application for your designs. However, the cloud functionality gives you access to your account, your designs, your elements, and everything within the Design Space from any device, anywhere in the world, so long as you have an internet connection and your account credentials.

Is my operating system compatible with Cricut Design Space?

Cricut Design Space is currently compatible with devices operating in the latest systems for Windows, Mac, Android, and iOS. If you have questions about your device's compatibility with the latest plugin for Cricut's Design Space, simply visit their page on system requirements and see what is listed there for you and the operating system you use.

https://help.cricut.com/hc/en-us/articles/360009556033-System-Requirements-Design-Space

Can I Use Design Space on My Chromebook?

Unfortunately, Cricut's Design Space isn't currently optimized for compatibility with the Chromebook operating system. This is because the need to download the plugin for the application is a current barrier for that operating system, but this isn't to say there is no possibility for compatibility in the near future.

Can I use the Design Space on more than one of my devices?

Yes, thanks to Cricut's web-based and cloud-based functionality, all of your designs, elements, fonts, purchases, and images are accessible from any device with an internet connection and your account credentials. This way, it's possible to start a design while you're out and about for the day, then wrap them up when you're back in your crafting space.

How many times can I use an image I buy in the Design Space?

Any design asset or element you purchase through the design space is yours to use as many times as you'd like while you have an active account with Cricut Design Space! Feel free to cut as many of every image you'd like!

I accidentally welded two images. How do I unweld them?

Unfortunately, there is no dedicated unweld option currently available in Design Space. If you weld an image, however, you can still click "Undo" if you have not saved the changes to your project. It is recommended that you save your images locally at each different stage, so you have clean images to work with for every project.

Can I disable the grid in Cricut Design Space?

Yes, Design Space allows you to toggle grid lines. On a Windows computer, or a Mac computer, open the "Account" menu.

This is the three stacked lines in the upper left-hand corner. Once you've clicked that, select Settings. You will see the Canvas Grid options and can select your preference. In the settings menu, you will also see Keyboard shortcuts. Select it to view a keyboard shortcut for toggling gridlines off and on.

When using the Design Space iOS App, the option for turning the gridlines off and on is available under Settings at the bottom of the screen. You may have to swipe left to view all of the options at the bottom of the screen.

How do I set design space to operate on the metric system?

On your computer (whether it's Windows or Mac), click the three stacked lines in the upper left-hand corner. From there, click "Settings." In those settings, you'll see the option to set inches or centimeters as the default measurement.

If you're using Design Space on your mobile device, you will access your settings from the bottom of your screen. You may need to scroll or swipe to the left to view all your options, but this setting is available on mobile as well!

What types of images can I upload through Cricut's design space iOS or Android apps?

Any images that are saved in the Photos or Gallery app on your Apple or Android device can be uploaded! If you have SVG files saved, you can upload those as well.

If you are trying to upload a .PDF or a .TIFF file, it should be noted that Cricut Design Space does not support these.

Can I upload images through the Android app?

Yes! Cricut understands how crucial mobile accessibility is to its users, so this feature has been made available on all platforms where you can access Cricut Design Space, including Android!

How do I delete images I uploaded through the mobile app?

This is another great feature that can be accessed through any available version of this platform, whether you have a Mac, PC, iOS, or Android device! In order to complete this task on your mobile device, open the design space app.

Select Upload in the bottom list of options, you may need to swipe to find it. Once you've tapped on that, select Open Uploaded Images. Once you're in your uploaded images, find the one you wish to delete. Tap the Info button, which is indicated with a green circle and a lowercase I. From here, you will be able to delete your image with ease!

Are the "despeckle" and "smooth" tools available in Design Space for Windows, Mac and Android?

At the time of writing, these features are exclusive to the iOS platform. This means that only Apple devices have this feature, and there is currently no indication as to whether or not this is intended to change in the future.

Can I upload photos while I'm offline?

Uploading images can only be done with an active high-speed internet connection. This is true of any platform you'll work with that is based on the web or the cloud. Once an image is uploaded, however, it can be accessed and downloaded onto other devices for offline use.

Is it possible for me to upload sewing patterns that I have made to Design Space?

If your sewing patterns are in any of the following formats, you will find that you can upload them to the Cricut Design Space! Accepted formats are: .SVG, .JPG, .BMP, .PNG, .GIF, .DXF.

It should be noted that SVG files retain their designed size when uploaded into the software, but all vectors are imported as cut lines. Then, once your image is uploaded, if your pattern contains pattern markings that should be drawn with a fabric pen, you will need to ensure that you change the relevant lines to write lines, and use the Attach tool so that they will write on your pieces where you need them to write.

What is SnapMat?

SnapMat is an iOS-exclusive feature that allows you to give yourself a virtual mat preview. This gives you the ability to line up your designs in Design Space, so they'll fit perfectly onto what you have laid on your mat. This feature allows you to place images and text over the snapshot of your mat so you can see exactly how your layout should be in the Design Space.

What Are the Advantages to Using SnapMat?

SnapMat gives you certainty in where your images will be placed when you send your design to cut through your Cricut. It will show you where your images will be drawn, cuts will be made, and how text lines up. With SnapMat, you can tell your Cricut to cut out a specific piece of a pattern you have stuck on your mat, write in specific areas of stationery, gift tags, envelopes, or cards, and you can get the absolute most out of your scraps and spare materials that are left from past projects!

Can I include multiple mats at one time with SnapMat?

SnapMat can only snap one mat at a time. If you'd like to snap multiple mats, you can do so individually, and work through your designs that way. This ensures that each mat is shot properly and that each one is done with precision.

Can I save the snaps of my mat from the SnapMat feature?

SnapMat doesn't currently have a "Save" feature for the images captured in it, so if you would like to retain a photo of your mat, simply take a screenshot in the middle of that process. This will save an image of your mat directly to your photo gallery.

If you find yourself referring to the image for where you have items on your may, it may be advisable to wait until you're ready to cut in order to take your snapshot.

How exact is SnapMat when it comes to where my cut lines will be?

The SnapMat technology is quite precise and the lines should be accurate to within a tiny fraction of an inch. If possible, it's best to give yourself as much room as you can to allow for small deviations, but you can trust that the lines are overall very close to where they ought to be.

How can I be sure that SnapMat will work with the Cricut mat I have?

SnapMat is compatible with all versions of the Cricut mats that are currently for sale. However, if you have a mat that is a bit older, or which has black gridlines, the app may have a little bit of a harder time differentiating between the grid and your design. It's best to do a couple of test runs with the mat you have, if it's not a Cricut brand mat, to ensure that everything will run smoothly.

What does it mean if SnapMat can't capture my mat?

The capture feature of the SnapMat application will automatically capture the picture of your mat, once it's within view and it can detect it. If your app isn't detecting the mat, there could be a few things you need to check. The positioning of the mat is key, so make sure that's done properly, your hand is completely steady, and make sure that there is nothing else in the shot. If you're still having trouble, try these tips:

Add Contrast to Your Mat

If SnapMat can't easily see the difference between the edges of your mat and the surface behind it, you might have difficulty getting the picture to snap. Try laying a darker piece of fabric or material behind the mat so it has a lot of contrast to work with and see if that solves it!

Let There be Light!

If the lighting in your space is too soft or if there isn't enough of it, your camera could be having trouble picking up on the mat that's in front of it. Try adding more light to your crafting space, ideally the light should be placed behind the camera, aimed at the mat. When you're working with intricate projects such as these, having good lighting is best for your eyes, anyway!

Flatten the Mat

If your mat has any curling, or if your mat is unable to lie flat for any reason, the curvature or different in depth could alter the camera's perception of where items are on your mat. If you need to flatten your mat, consider placing it between to very heavy objects to flatten it.

Mind the Edges of Your Grid

The edges of your grid are part of what tell the SnapMat application where the materials are on your mat. So if you have materials that are hanging over the sides of your grid, you might find that your app is having trouble picking up where items are on your mat, or how large your mat actually is.

Look for the Green Square

Once SnapMat detects the edges around your mat, you'll see the green square or rectangle that indicates it's snapping the picture. If you're not seeing that rectangle, the picture has not been captured and further troubleshooting may be needed.

Keep it Level

The blue circles in the SnapMat application are a level. If you use those, ensure that the circles are even and this will tell you if your phone is level and thus, picking up a completely level and true photo of the mat in front of it. This will help you to be sure all the materials on your mat are captured in the right proportions.

Mind the Size of your Mat

In your settings, you can select the 12" x 12" mat, or the 12" x 24" mat. Be sure to choose the one that you're using so your entire design is captured. This will help you to get all of the materials on the mat cut in one swoop when you're ready to load it into your Cricut Machine!

My hands shake; how can I use SnapMat?

Don't worry, keeping the camera steady can be a real pain for a lot of users, so we've figured out a way around that. Many crafters have solved this by placing their mat on the floor, just under the edge of their table, while resting the phone or device on the tabletop, with the camera hanging over the edge. In most cases, this keeps your phone so steady that the snap is completed in mere seconds.

What is offline mode for Cricut Design Space?

This is a feature that is exclusively available through the iOS platform. With this feature, you can download your items for use in an offline environment later. This is ideal if you're planning on working on your designs in a space that does not have an active internet connection for an extended period of time. In that time, you can still work on your designs without worrying about losing those creative thoughts!

What is available to download for offline use?

Every element or asset that you personally own, or for which you've purchased rights through Cricut Design Space is available to download for offline use. This includes images that you've uploaded from other devices, images or assets that you've obtained through an active Cricut Access membership. It is up to you to hand pick what assets you would like to make available for offline use.

How do I save projects so I can use them offline?

This step can only be done with an active internet connection, so make sure you download before you go offline. Open a project you wish to save for offline use and select the "Save As" option. Select the "Save to this iPad/iPhone" option and this will allow you to use that project at a later time with no connection.

How do I save changes to my projects while offline?

When you're working on a project in offline mode, simply tap "Save," and the file you have saved to your device will automatically be updated, without having to reselect the "Save to this iPad/iPhone" option if there is no internet connection.

Can I download images for later, offline use?

While you have an active internet connection, you can download images to your device for later, offline use. To do this, open the "Images" screen, select an image, and tap "Download." The image label will indicate when this is done and the image will immediately be available, regardless of an internet connection.

How many images can I download?

Cricut Design Space does not impose a limit on the total number of images you can download in one day. You can only select 50 images to be downloaded at one time, but there is no limit to how many times you can repeat this process in one sitting. With this feature, you'll have access to all you need when you're offline!

What does the "Select Visible" button do?

The "Select Visible" button that's located at the bottom of the "Images" screen will select all the images that are currently on the screen you're looking at. This feature can help you to quickly group images for fast download with as little hassle as humanly possible!

Where can I look at my downloads?

To view your downloaded images, go to the "Images" screen. Once you're there, tap the "Filter" icon, select the "On this iPad/iPhone" option and all the images displayed will be all the images that are stored locally. If you're currently in offline mode, then this will be your default view of the "Images" screen.

Can I download fonts to use offline?

Yes! Fonts are among the assets you can download to your device for later, offline use! Here's how to download your font to your device:

- Tap the "Text" button
- Once the font view pops up, tap the "Select" button in the upper left-hand corner
- Tap on your desired fonts to select them
- Tap "Download" in the upper right-hand corner of the screen

Now that you've followed these steps, these fonts are available for offline use on your iOS device!

How do I look at all the projects I've saved to my device?

To see this, tap the "Menu" button, which looks like three stacked bars. This will be at the top of the "Projects" screen. Once there, tap the option that says, "My Projects on this iPad/iPhone." If you're already offline, this will be your default view of the "Projects" screen.

Can I save Ready-to-Make projects to my device?

If you'd like to save a Ready-to-Make project to your device so you can use it offline, you can save it to your device. This is done by picking "Customize," tapping "Save As," then selecting "Save to this iPad/iPhone."

It is important to note that project photos and instructions will not be saved offline. If you need these, it could be beneficial to take screenshots of those aspects or print them off so you can refer to them while you're working in offline mode.

Is there a limit to how long my offline images are available to me?

Free images gotten through the Cricut Design Space (including basic shapes) can be used for seven consecutive days without refreshing the internet connection. Permissions will expire after that time, but can easily be renewed by connecting to the internet and relaunching the Cricut Design Space application.

I bought images with Cricut Access; are they available offline?

Yes, the images that you bought with your Cricut Access membership can be downloaded while your membership is active. This means that images in that category can be used without an internet connection for up to 30 days, or until the subscription needs to be renewed, whichever comes first. At that time, you'll be prompted to reconnect your device to the internet so you can renew your subscription and your license to keep using those images offline.

Can I delete items I've downloaded?

Absolutely, simply go to "Images," and, if you're online, select the "Images saved to this iPad/iPhone," and delete with the

"Remove" button that populates. It should be noted that if an image that was not downloaded is selected by mistake, the "Remove" button will simply be a "Download" button.

Do my projects automatically sync with the cloud when I sign back online?

No, you will need to manually save each of your projects to your "Projects" page, taking care to overwrite older versions of your work, if that is what you wish to do with them.

Can I update my projects in the cloud with offline changes?

Yes, simply save your projects to the "Projects" screen with the same exact name as the previous version of your project. This will completely overwrite the project you currently have saved to the cloud with the changes you made while you were offline.

What sort of things can't I do in Offline Mode?

Features that are only available online are Print then Cut calibration, custom materials, setup for a new machine, cartridge and category views, and image upload services. If you wish to do any of these things, simply connect your device to the internet and you may do so without issue.

Is offline mode available on desktop?

No, at this time the offline mode function is exclusively available for iOS devices. There are no indications at this time, as to whether or not Cricut intends to add other platforms to this functionality.

Can I download an entire cartridge to use in offline mode?

It's not possible to download an entire cartridge of content in one move, but you are able to download as much of the individual assets as you like from any cartridge or category.

What happens if I sign out of my app?

Every asset you manipulate in any way is associated with your Cricut ID, which is attached to the cloud. What this means is that, when you sign out of the app after you've downloaded something, you will need to log into the app again with an internet connection to access those assets, projects, images, etc., once again.

It is important to note that signing out of the app can only be done when you have an active internet connection, so there is no way to mistakenly do this while you're stick in offline mode.

If you delete the Cricut app from your device, even while in offline mode, any assets that were downloaded from the app will be removed from your device, and the only way to get them back is to sign back into the app with a live internet connection, and download them all over again.

With the Move and Hide feature in the print layout, if I move an image to a different color mat, does it affect my layout on the canvas?

Nope! Any changes made on the mat do not affect the canvas in any way.

Using Move and Hide, can I move printable images to another mat?

At this time, printable images cannot be moved to another mat.

In Move and Hide, it is possible to move multiple images to a new mat all at once?

Currently this feature is only available on mobile iOS devices. Selecting an image, tapping and holding on other images to select them as well, multiple images can be moved at once. There is no indication as to whether this feature will be made available on other devices and platforms in the near future.

How many images can I move to one mat?

There is not currently a limit to the number of images you can put onto a mat. If they fit, you're all clear!

Can I save money by hiding images from the mat?

The price of a project does not update to reflect whether or not images have been hidden. If the image has been included in the design in any capacity, you will incur the charge for that element.

Can I save the layout of my mat?

Mat layouts cannot currently be saved. When you return to your canvas, the changes made to all your mats will be reset. If you need to remember the layout, try taking a screenshot!

Is Cricut Design Space compatible with the current version of my internet browser?

Microsoft has begun to phase out Internet Explorer. As such, it is not up to date or able to keep up with the components of Cricut Design Space. Check the Cricut website for the most up-to-date information on system and browser requirements. At the time of writing, however, the latest versions of the following browsers are compatible with Cricut Design Space.

- Apple Safari
- Google Chrome
- Microsoft Edge
- Mozilla Firefox

If you are switching over to one of these browsers from Internet Explorer, take the time to familiarize yourself with it, get your bookmarks and favorites imported, and then visit design.cricut.com to download the plugin. From here, setup with your machine will be a breeze and you'll be off and crafting in no time!

What Features are Available on Which Apps?

Here is a handy chart that lays out exactly what features are available in the Cricut Design Space, as well as what platforms support each feature! Be sure to consult this chart if you're weighing the options of which platform to get for your crafting experience.

Feature	Desktop Computer	iOS App	Android App
3D layer visualization		✓	
Attach	✓	✓	✓
Bluetooth compatible	✓	✓	✓
Contour	✓	✓	✓
Curve Text	✓		
Cut & write in one step	✓	✓	✓
Flatten to print	✓	✓	✓
Image upload	✓	✓	✓
Knife Blade cutting	✓		
Link Physical Cartridges	✓		
Machine setup	✓	✓	✓
Offline		✓	
Pattern fills	✓		
Photo Canvas		✓	
Print then cut	✓	✓	
Slice and weld	✓	✓	✓
Smart Guides		✓	✓
SnapMat		✓	
System fonts	✓	✓	✓
Templates	✓		
Writing style fonts	✓	✓	✓

How can I keep my Cricut mats sticky for longer?

When you buy a new Cricut mat, you will find a semi-rigid piece of clear plastic that comes adhered to the front of it. If you save this piece of plastic, you can put it back on top of your mat after each project, to ensure that nothing will stick to it in between your projects. This will keep things like pet hair, glitter, paper scraps, and dust from getting stuck to and compromising the adhesion of your Cricut mat!

Is there anywhere else to get weeding tools?

Harbor Freight and other similar hardware stores sell sets of hooks that are similar to the weeding tool that Cricut has to offer. These sets of weeding hooks generally have a very low price point and do the job just as well as Cricut's proprietary weeding hooks. If you find that this is a tool you use a lot of need to replace often, consider looking at Harbor Freight or another hardware retailer for a suitable replacement on a budget and in bulk!

How should I weed my more intricate designs?

There is a technique for more intricate designs known as Reverse Weeding. This is a technique that is often done on vinyl when a design with a lot of very thin or curly parts are implemented in the design. Once you've run the vinyl through, stick the transfer tape to the front of the design before doing *any* weeding.

Use your scraper to full burnish the transfer tape down onto the vinyl design. This will help it to adhere to it so nothing unnecessary comes up when you get to the weeding stage of this hack.

Once you've done this, peel all of it away from the contact paper, then make use of your weeding tool to remove to the excess vinyl from the transfer tape. This has been found to eliminate a lot of tearing and stretching that can occur with projects like this.

Once all the excess is removed from your design, burnish it like normal onto your design piece, and then remove the transfer tape just like you would otherwise.

My mats keep curling when they're stored. How should I store them?

It has been found, amongst many crafters in the community, that utilizing wall space and command hooks is the best way to store the Cricut craft mats. It keeps them from slipping behind your furniture, getting lost in stacks on your table, or getting damaged in the shuffle.

If you keep them hung up on the wall, they're always kept straight and safe, and they're always right where you need them to be.

Do I have any alternatives when it comes to transfer tape?

One hack that a number of craters, bloggers, and YouTubers swear by is buying contact paper from either Target or the Dollar Tree and using it at transfer tape! Contact paper is available nearly everywhere and you can get a lot of it for a very reasonable price. The adhesive on contact paper is meant to be removed after months or even years of use with little to no residue. This quality makes it a great substitute for transfer tape, which we rely on to keep all our project pieces exactly in place between the carrier sheet and our project materials!

How do I sharpen my Cricut's blades?

A very popular Cricut trick in use is to stick a clean, fresh piece of foil to your Cricut mat, and run it through with the blade you with to sharpen. Running the blades through the thin metal helps to revitalize their edges and give them a little extra staying power until it's time to buy replacements.

Another way to do this is to make a ball of foil, remove the blades from the housing, and stick them into the ball of foil several times, until you notice a shine on the blade. This can give you a better idea of how sharpened your blades are becoming before you finish up with them, and it seems like a more expedient way to sharpen several blades in one sitting, but the reviews seem to be equally as positive as letting your machine do the work for you on one blade at a time.

My mat isn't quite as sticky as it used to be. How do I keep my projects in place?

You'll find that as time goes on, your mat will slowly lose its grip on your projects in some places. Before giving up and throwing your mat out when it still has some of the grip left on it, consider using masking tape or painter's tape to keep your projects in place. This will hold the materials in place while they're being cut, but the adhesive isn't strong enough to damage your project or mat, and it won't leave a residue.

Having a fresh mat with a strong grip can be an invaluable asset in your crafting and it makes your projects go so smoothly.

Having that grip on the mat is like having an extra set of hands while you're trying to work. However, the realists in the crafting community know that it's not always possible to replace your mats as soon as they begin to lose their grip.

How can I adhere my designs to a rounded surface with no bubbles or wrinkles?

If you're transferring a decal onto something that is rounded, like a cup or mug, you will find it much easier to lay the decal flat if you cut intermittent slits in the transfer tape. While this does make it harder to reuse that bit of tape, you will find that they'll lie down on the surface much more readily this way.

How do you see your cut lines in the glitter iron on material?

Due to the nature of glittery iron-on deflecting light in every which direction, finding your cut lines can be really difficult and the weeding can take a little bit of extra tie as a result. However, if you use a small amount of baby powder and brush it across the back of your design, you will see those cut lines much more clearly.

You only need a very small amount of powder for this and you will find that the powder doesn't interfere with the design or its adhesion in any way!

Is there an organized way to store my material scraps?

One of the many beautiful things about organized people is that they love telling other people how they can be organized! The internet Cricut community has recently blown up with this hack. Keep a binder with page protectors, and use those protectors as pockets for all your material scraps of paper-size or smaller.

For just a couple dollars, you can organize your scraps in any way you choose, keep them all together, and never worry if they've gotten to wrinkled or damaged to be used in your future projects!

Cricut Hacks

Pegboard Tool Storage

Each proprietary Cricut tool you have comes equipped with a very handy eyelet at the end of the tool. This makes it very easy to store their accessories by hanging them up. In a crafting space, a pegboard makes hanging up your tools in your crafting space so unbelievably easy.

Right over your space, you can have all your tools organized and laid out right before your eyes. No more digging through drawers or boxes, no scuffing up your tools, and no worrying about during or chipping any edges.

The more accessible your tools are, the easier I have found it to be for inspiration for amazing projects to hit me!

IKEA Grocery Bag Holders as Material Organizers

IKEA offers very reasonably priced plastic dispensers for grocery bags that feature symmetrically placed circular slots. This makes them ideal for holding several rolls of Cricut materials each. They cost only $2.99 each and, with one or two of them, you can keep all your rolls of material from folding, creasing, wrinkling, or otherwise getting damaged.

Plus, with how cute all the materials are, they make a pretty great decorative piece on their own!

Use a Lint Roller

Once I explain this one a little bit, it might seem a little bit obvious, but I promise it really is a life saver that can save you a lot of trouble as well as keep the grip strength on your mat. As you do more and more projects, little bits of dust and debris will find their way onto your mat. As they do, you'll notice a buildup of dust, debris, paper scraps, glitter, fabric and more. Since *Cricut strongly urges against cleaning your mats* in order to preserve the grip on them, it is imperative to exercise proper care to make them last.

A large number of crafters have sworn by this technique and suggest that it has added weeks to the lives of their Cricut mats. However, since Cricut does not endorse any attempts to improve the lasting power of the grip on their mats, it is best to hold off on trying this hack until you're sure you'd need a new mat anyway so that, if it doesn't work well, you can get a new one without feeling like you've lost anything.

Lint rollers from the dollar store or the dollar section as Target will work just fine for this hack, so there is no need to break the bank on getting yourself a lint roller for this task, either!

Use Non-Alcohol Wipes to Clean your Mats

Since Cricut **strongly urges against cleaning your mats**, it is imperative that you realize that you do this at your own risk. However, a good number of people have tested this hack and found it to be a great way to give their mats a couple extra weeks of life.

Since Cricut does not endorse any attempts to improve the lasting power of the grip on their mats, it is best to hold off on trying this hack until you're sure you'd need a new mat anyway so that, if it doesn't work well, you can get a new one without feeling like you've lost anything.

Using baby wipes or non-alcohol wipes on your mats can remove things that are stuck in the grip of your mat, clear away dirt or paper leavings, and can give you back a couple extra weeks of grip strength in your mats!

Wash Your Mats with Soap, Water, and a Gentle Scrubber

Since Cricut **strongly urges against cleaning your mats**, it is imperative that you realize that you do this at your own risk. However, a large number of Cricut crafters have said that this little tip has saved them from having to buy a new mat for an extra couple weeks at least.

Since Cricut does not endorse any attempts to improve the lasting power of the grip on their mats, it is best to hold off on trying this hack until you're sure you'd need a new mat anyway so that, if it doesn't work well, you can get a new one without feeling like you've lost anything.

Using warm water (don't go too hot, or you could melt the adhesive on your mat) and a mild dish soap like Dawn, Fairy, or Palmolive, and the soft side of a kitchen sponge, you can gently scrub the adhesive grip side of your mat. Don't apply too much pressure, as you don't want to grind debris further in, or just scrub the adhesive off of the mat entirely.

Once you've done this, thoroughly rinse the mat and pat dry with a linen dishtowel, or a high quality paper towel that won't leave behind any debris. Once you've done this, set the mat to dry completely for an hour or two and then give it a shot to see how much the wash helped you out.

Doing all these hacks over time will give you a feel for what works, what doesn't, and how frequently you really need to replace your Cricut mats.

Clean your Blades

After some time of repeated use, you might find that your blades are snagging on your materials or that the cuts aren't as crisp as you might light for them to be. If you're dealing with this, remove the housing from its accessory clamp, and press the button at the top of the housing. This will extend the blade outside of the housing, but will also give you a safe grip on the blade while you're cleaning it.

If there is any gunk visible on the blade, using a very deliberate grip with your opposing thumb and forefinger, pinch around the shaft of the blade and pull down, make sure not to go against the angle of the blade as you do. This should remove any foreign materials from the tip of your blade, making your cuts more precise.

You can also take a ball of tin foil and poke the blade into the ball a few times, which will remove debris while also doing a mild sharpening on them.

Leave the Material Dial on your Explore Set to Custom

One of the problems that a lot of Cricut Explore users have is remembering to set the dial on the top of their machine for the correct material they've loaded into the machine. If you do this, you might find that your blade is pushing too hard or not hard enough for the material that you've loaded into it.

It's very common to leave your machine on the setting that you used last, which can then cause troubles while you're doing your next one. As a solution for this problem, a lot of crafters are making it a habit to set their dial to "Custom," at the end of each project, as you won't know what material you could be using with your Cricut next.

Leaving your dial set to "Custom" will cause the Cricut software to ask you what type of material is in the machine at the beginning of every single project. This eliminates the possibility of ever cutting too much or too little due to this issue.

Remind Yourself

If you don't think that leaving your machine on "Custom" is the solution for you, or if you have trouble remembering to do that part, make a craft project for yourself! Make a vinyl decal that will remind you to turn the dial at the beginning of your projects, and burnish it onto the side of your Cricut Explore machine!

Bonus Hack: Don't forget to cut slits in the edges of your transfer tape so you can go along the curved edges!

Test it Out

If you're about to do a large project, a project with a lot of intricate cuts, or a project on a material you've never used in the past, do yourself a favor and **_run a test_**.

Set your machine to cut just a simple shape from that material on the settings that you'd like to use and make sure that your blades are sharp enough, the settings are firm enough, and that the material is right for your machine.

Doing this will eliminate waiting for a project to be completed, only to find that half the lines didn't come out right. This is a waste of time, effort, money, and heartache!

Flip Your Canvas

Painting canvases, or canvas that is mounted on a wooden frame, has a great big hollow spot in the middle. That wooden frame it's mounted on creates that big hollow spot, onto which you can't apply pressure. Putting pressure on that spot in the canvas could stretch it, thus making your designs uneven, not sitting properly, or just wonky in general.

The best way to get your design burnished onto a canvas will require a change of method. Once you have the transfer tape layered on your canvas with your design, all properly positioned where it's meant to be, then you will want to give it a preliminary once-over with the burnishing tool so it will stick, then flip your canvas so your design is face down on your work space.

Now that it's upside down, you're going to burnish the back of your canvas. Give it a thorough rub with your burnishing tool on the back of the canvas, in the center of that wood frame, and apply all the pressure you need to get your design to stick on the bumpy texture of your canvas. This allows you to apply that pressure, without compromising the tautness of your canvas.

Once your design is fully burnished, you can flip it back over, remove the transfer tape, and admire your handiwork! If you need help getting that transfer tape to come up off the canvas without your work sticking to it, see the next hack in this section.

Roll Your Transfer Tape

Sometimes, you will find that a surface is more apt to let a design stick to the transfer tape when you're trying to remove it. The best tip I've found for getting around this is by using the XL Scraper tool from Cricut. Peel up the first corner of your design and place the XL Scraper, round side up, right at the fold of the tape you're removing.

As you remove the tape, continue to push the XL Scraper into the crease of your transfer tape as it's being pulled up. This will help encourage the letters and lines of your design to stay put on your surface as you remove the transfer tape!

In my experience, this hack has come most in handy with surfaces like canvas, wood, or slate. If it's a rough or porous surface, you should bank on needing to use this method to remove your transfer tape. It will make your life a lot easier.

Use Heat to Encourage Sticking

If you're using a porous material such as slate, wood, or canvas and your vinyl doesn't quite seem like it's going to stay where it should, get out your trusty hair dryer or heat gun!

Because the materials for your Cricut are not very robust materials, you aren't going to want to use a ton of heat with them. You just want to give them enough heat that the adhesive starts to grip the crannies of the surface under your design. Melting your design could drastically change the way it looks or do damage to it, which is not what we want.

In order to mitigate the heat on your design, try to keep the heat source moving over your design. Don't focus the heat in any one spot, and hold the heat gun or hair dryer a good distance from the surface.

Go for the Straightener

If you have a decal that you've made with iron-on vinyl, and you're looking to put that design on a uniquely-shaped item, your best bet for applying heat to get that design to stay on your item just might be your hair straightener.

Your straightener can apply heat to a small space, is easily maneuverable and has less of a chance of burning or melting plastic components of the item you're looking to iron your decal onto.

Use Parchment Paper Instead of Teflon Sheets

If you're like me and had never even heard of Teflon sheets before looking into Cricut as a craft, you will be relieved to find that the parchment paper you can get in bulk in the baking aisle at the grocery store will serve just fine.

This paper is only used as a buffer between your iron-on designs and the heat source that you're using. It helps to prevent scorching and melting, and parchment paper does an excellent job at diffusing heat.

Use caution when you use this method, however, as putting too much heat on the paper in one spot for a prolonged period *could* burn it or cause scorching.

This is one of those in-a-pinch tips that will get you through a few projects, but Teflon sheets are the best, safest item to use for iron-on decals.

Put Water in That Glass

If you're trying to put a decal on the outside of a vase, drinking glass, shot glass, jar, etc., put some water in it. This will act as your level and will tell you how high up your design should be, and will help you to keep all your design elements level.

Be sure there is no liquid on the outside of the glass before you adhere your design! You wouldn't want to ruin it.

Invert Your Pens

The Cricut pens you can put in accessory clamp A should be stored upside down. This will help all the ink in the pen to store down near the tip, will keep the tip from drying out, and will give you clean, crisp lines every time you use them, no matter how long it's been. Don't worry about having to shake your markers, soak them, or replace them with this hack!

Branch out with your Markers

Certain members of the Cricut community have said that they have found other brands of markers, particularly Crayola, to be excellent replacement markers for their Cricut system. You can get more variety in terms of color and style, without the prohibitive cost or options that the Cricut brand has to offer. Try several different brands and see what works for you!

Use Rubber Pen Grips

When you're looking to use markers that aren't the Cricut brand, you might find that the pens aren't quite big enough around to clip properly into accessory clamp A. In such an event, get some of those rubber or silicone pencil grips that aren't curved on the outside, and slide one around your marker. Doing so might make it big enough around to improve your experience!

In a Pinch, Use a Hair Tie

If you find that you have a pen you would like to use with clamp A, but you don't have a pencil grip on hand, wrap a hair tie around the grip area a few times and try that on for size!

You may need to try a couple different times to get the fit exactly right, but this will often do the trick for keeping a non-Cricut pen in place in clamp A!

Pigeonhole Your Strong Grip Transfer Tape

Cricut's transfer tapes are available with varying strengths of grip. The Strong Grip transfer tape truly lives up to its name. When you're using transfer tape with your designs, if the adhesive is too strong, it could stretch or harm your design, and no one wants that.

This transfer tape is not, however, without its uses. It is my recommendations that you use your strong grip transfer tape *exclusively* on vinyl that is coated with glitter. The extra grip will help the vinyl to stick to the transfer tape, without harming any portion of the design as you're working.

The glitter gives the surface of the vinyl a coarse surface that can make it hard for tape to hold onto. This tape will hold onto that material, but it won't hurt your designs. Other transfer tapes seem to have a hard time sticking to that glittery surface, but the glitter vinyl and Cricut's Strong Grip Transfer Tape seem to be a match made in heaven!

Weaken Your Transfer Tape

If you find yourself in a pinch with a transfer tape that is stronger than what you need for the project you're doing, you might want to take a couple minutes to weaken it. This is very simply done by peeling the transfer tape away from its carrier sheet or backing, and applying the transfer tape to a cloth surface like linen or your jeans. Something that won't leave a ton of fibers behind, but that will weaken that adhesive.

Washi Setting for Intricate Designs

If you're making a very intricate or delicate design on vinyl, you might find that your blade isn't being quite as delicate as it needs to be for the task at hand. If this is the case, use the "Washi Tape" or "Washi Sheet" setting for your cuts. Washi tape and washi sheets are a very delicate material and the settings on your machine reflect this. This should get you those delicate results you're looking for. Don't forget to reverse weed your more delicate projects to keep those fine and intricate lines intact!

Strong Grip Lint Roller

If you are a crafter who does a lot of projects with the pink mat, which is meant specifically to hold fabric, you might find that a good deal of fabric debris and fibers gets stuck to the mat over time. If this is the case, take some of the Strong Grip Transfer Tape and place is sticky side down on your pink mat.

Do this several times over the entire surface of your mat to remove that fiber and debris. Try doing this after working with felt, flannel, wool, burlap and other fabrics that have a lot of fibers. You should find that doing this will remove a good deal of the unwanted debris from your mat, leaving tat strong grip behind to continue doing its best work for you in your crafting!

Remove Bubbles in Your Vinyl Designs

If you find that you've got bubbles in your vinyl, roll the rounded back of the scraper over the design to push them toward the outer edges. For very stubborn air bubbles, you may find that you need to use a fine blade to pop the bubbles and smooth them down with your finger or scraping tool. The rubber roller is also a good help in situations such as these!

Give Your Transfer Tape a Good Rubdown

If you find that a design has a lot of bubbles in it, return the transfer tape over the design and give it a *really* thorough burnishing. Doing so should help you to work out any air bubbles that had appeared, without causing streaks or scratches on your design.

It's important to burnish really thoroughly and look for bubbles and wrinkles before removing the transfer tape in the first place. This is the perfect time to burnish away without worrying about scuffing the design, so go nuts!

Remove Your Transfer Tape at an Angle

The best way to eliminate the possibility of creating bubbles or wrinkles in your design is to peel up one corner of your transfer tape and remove it all by pulling upward or downward at an angle. Pulling straight upward could put air between your design and the crafting surface. When using this method, you can also use your XL Scraper to keep your letters down, as described in one of the tips above. This will help keep your letters on even ground when negative pressure is applied while removing the transfer tape!

Iron-On Material Works Great with Wood

If working with wood is interesting to you and you like making plaques and other beautiful wooden designs, you might consider trying iron-on vinyl. The thickness of the material and the strong grip it creates when heat is applied makes it a great candidate for sticking fast onto a porous surface.

A word of caution with this method, be sure that the iron never comes in direct contact with the wooden surface, or you could end up damaging the wood through moisture or scorching! Keep your Teflon sheets handy and iron on in bursts if you need to!

Don't Remove Your Design from the Mat Before Weeding

"Weed on the mat!" This is a common phrase you will hear thrown your way my Cricut crafters who are looking to help new crafters who are getting used to Cricut. A common mistake made by new crafters is to remove the vinyl from the Cricut mat before starting the weeding process. However, weeding your design on the mat makes things way easier on you. Think of that grip like an extra pair of hands that keeps your design right where it needs to be while you weed. **Weed on the mat!**

Use a Lint Roller to Weed Your Cardstock

When you have a cardstock design on your mat that has just been cut, weeding it can take a little bit of extra time. However, if you use a lint roller, the cardstock excess will stick to the lint roller. With practice, this method can cut your weeding time in half with all of your cardstock projects!

In a Pinch, Use a Fork

If you find yourself in the middle of a project and you can't find your weeding tool or if your weeding tool has broken, a fork can be an unlikely substitute! This mostly works on vinyl, and toothpicks are another suitable replacement that you might find to be more effective! Try a couple of other implements and see what works best for you in your crafting!

Save Your Old Gift Card

If you don't have your scraper or burnishing tool handy, using an old or leftover gift card is a great stand-in! The flat edges, and small shape are very helpful for smoothing down edges, working out bubbles, scraping up stuck edges, working in creases or crevices, and everything your scraping tool is good for! Don't get me wrong, the Cricut scraping tool is worth its weight in gold, and then some. It is an ideal tool for all its various purposes, but in a pinch, a gift card should get the job done with a little more finesse and elbow grease!

Use Fabric Barrier for Your Iron-Ons

When ironing on a decal that you've made, using a Teflon sheet is usual. This helps to diffuse and evenly distribute the heat so there's no scorching from the iron on the decal. However, this same effect can be achieved if you use a regular cotton fabric and keep the iron moving.

Don't allow the iron to come to rest on the decal, because too much heat could get through. Utilizing this method can help you to achieve your ironed on result with little to no damage in the event that you don't have a Teflon sheet on hand for your craft!

Using a cotton fabric in place of Teflon can be a temporary measure until you decide if iron-on is something you'll work with regularly! Once you're committed to that craft, then you can spend the money on a Teflon sheet!

Pump Up the Pressure

As your blades begin to lose their sharp edge, you can increase the pressure in your Cricut settings to get the most out of your blades before sharpening or replacing them! This is a great way to ensure you're using your blades to their fullest capacity before removing or replacing them!

Add a Placeholder Shape in Design Space

Once you've begun to gather scraps of the materials from your projects, you will find it's not as simple to line up your materials on your mat. You might end up with some wonky shapes, or some shapes that just aren't the width you're accustomed to having on your mat. The best way to make sure your current design will fit on the piece you have is to line it up in the corner of the mat you intend to use for your project.

Once you have it on the mat, use the measurements to tell you how big the piece is. Make a blank square in Cricut Design Space that is roughly the size of the piece you have on your mat. The Design Space has dimensions in it that can easily be adjusted to what you need.

Once you have that shape in the Design Space, just use it as a scale for your project to ensure that what you have will fit on the materials available to you!

Heat Makes Vinyl Easier to Remove

If you've applied a vinyl decal to a surface, but it didn't quite come out the way you wanted it to, don't panic. With a heat gun or a hair dryer, you can loosen the adhesive enough that you can remove the decal or reposition it.

Be warned that the removal process might not be as gentle on the decal, so don't depend on being able to reapply it. But hey, stranger things have happened, right? In the world of crafting, nothing is impossible!

You Can Reuse Transfer Tape

If you're careful and store your transfer tape with the carrier sheet or protective backing, you can reuse good transfer tape up to seven times before the adhesive is no longer strong enough to carry over your projects! Throwing out your transfer tape after one use will cost you a lot of money, and you'll just get sick of driving to the craft store over and over again! Find a brand of transfer tape you like, stock up, and take as long to get through each piece as you possibly can!

This is the ultimate tip for getting your money's worth with a material you absolutely cannot live without as a Cricut crafter!

Mind the Cap

When your Cricut pens or other type of pen is in use in accessory clamp A, put the cap on the back of the pen so you don't lose it! With crafting projects that involve so many small, losable parts, it's best to wrangle any and all accessories you can, as you go!

Maintenance

After a while, you may notice some of your projects coming out in a condition that is less-than-crisp. In this section, I'll outline a troubleshooting and maintenance checklist you can utilize to bring your Cricut machine back into peak working condition!

1. Ensure your machine is on stable footing.

This may seem pretty basic but ensuring that your machine is on a level surface will allow it to make more precise cuts every single time. Rocking of the machine or wobbling could cause unstable results in your projects.

Ensure no debris has gotten stuck under the feet of your machine that could cause instability before proceeding to the next troubleshooting step!

2. Redo all Cable Connections

So, your connections are in the best possible working order, undo all your cable connection, blow into the ports or use canned air, and then securely plug everything back into the right ports. This will help to make sure all the connections are talking to each other where they should be!

3. Completely Dust and Clean Your Machine

Your little Cricut works hard for you! Return the favor by making sure you're not allowing gunk, dust, grime, or debris to build up in the surfaces and crevices. Adhesive can build up on the machine around the mat input and on the rollers, so be sure to focus on those areas!

If you have a can of compressed air, use it to blast any small parts and pieces of material or dust that may have built up around the **cutting strip, bar and rollers,** and **mat input**. Q-Tips can also be a great resource for cleaning out the small spaces in your machine; put that rubbing alcohol to further use!

4. Check Your Blade Housing

Sometimes debris and leavings from your materials can build up inside the housings for your blades! Open them up and clear any built-up materials that could be impeding swiveling or motion.

5. Sharpen Your Blades

A very popular Cricut trick in use is to stick a clean, fresh piece of foil to your Cricut mat, and run it through with the blade you with to sharpen. Running the blades through the thin metal helps to revitalize their edges and give them a little extra staying power until it's time to buy replacements.

Another way to do this is to make a ball of foil, remove the blades from the housing, and stick them into the ball of foil several times, until you notice a shine on the blade. This can give you a better idea of how sharpened your blades are becoming before you finish up with them, and it seems like a more expedient way to sharpen several blades in one sitting, but the reviews seem to be equally as positive as letting your machine do the work for you on one blade at a time.

Conclusion

Thank you for making it through to the end of *Cricut for Beginners*, let's hope it was informative and able to provide you with all of the tools you need to achieve your goals whatever they may be.

The next step is to find projects and materials that excite you and dive right in! I would love to see my readers embrace the vast number of crafting opportunities that now lie ahead of them.

There really is no limit to the amazing things you can do with the tools you've purchased for this craft. They're so versatile and, with your creative power added to that versatility, the sky is the limit!

Finally, if you found this book useful in any way, a review on Amazon is always appreciated!

Description

Cricut for Beginners is the unofficial guide that will take you from choosing your very first Cricut machine, through setup, all the way through the intermediate skill level. If you are an experienced Cricut user, the information in this book can serve as an essential reference on the best care and troubleshooting tips, as well as ideas that are outside of the box.

There is no information in this book that wouldn't be considered absolutely essential to the Cricut crafter of any skill level. In the pages of this book, we've covered all the specifics of using the Cricut Design Space to the fullest, and to using everything you've created and curated to make breathtaking projects.

Getting acquainted with a new web application and new hardware has never been as simple and intuitive as it is with the latest models on the Cricut product line, and with the breakdowns provided in these chapters. Anyone can learn how the machine and the software work, make the most of them, and come out the other side with even more ideas on how to use the system.

This should be between 300 and 500 words

- Full descriptions of each of the machines currently available on the Cricut product line, what they do, how they differ, and which one best suits your purposes as a crafter.

- Step-by-step guides on several different types of crafts that you can do with your Cricut, right out of the box, as well as tips on how to make them truly unique to you and your style.

- The most pressing questions asked by crafters in the Cricut community, and answers that will definitively solve all your problems and more.

- Hacks to save your machine, your wallet, and your time. You won't find a more comprehensive list of Cricut hacks anywhere else!

- A comprehensive list of 100 materials you can use with your Cricut system to create beautiful, dynamic projects for any occasion.

Cricut for Beginners is the guide you need to get you started on creating unique, dynamic, breathtaking crafts for any and every occasion. Crafts for decoration and crafts for practical use are all part of this comprehensive guide, so whatever you're looking to learn, we've got you covered!

Show off your creative side through crafts for the workplace, uniquely created items that can make your job easier, or even embellishments for your wardrobe. No matter how you'd like to show the world your creative side, Cricut is the tool to help you do it!

Happy crafting!

Made in the USA
Middletown, DE
26 December 2019